THE SUPERNATURAL TRANSFORMATION SERIES

Volume II

THE NEW CREATION MIRACLE

THE FOUNDATION OF THE HEART REVOLUTION

© **Phil Mason**

THE NEW CREATION MIRACLE

Unless otherwise identified, all Scripture citations are from the NEW KING JAMES VERSION © 1982 Thomas Nelson inc. Used by permission.

Scripture quotations identified as (KJV) are taken from the Holy Bible, King James Version Public Domain

Scripture quotations marked (NIV) are taken from the Holy Bible, New International Version®. Copyright © 1973, 1978, 1984 by Biblica, Inc.™ Used by permission of Zondervan. All rights reserved worldwide. www.zondervan.com

Scripture quotations marked (NLT) are taken from the Holy Bible, New Living Translation, copyright 1996. Used by permission of Tyndale House Publishers, Inc., Wheaton, Illinois 60189. All rights reserved.

Scripture quotations marked (NASB) are taken from the New American Standard Bible®, Copyright © 1960, 1962, 1963, 1968, 1971, 1972, 1973, 1975, 1977, 1995 by The Lockman Foundation. Used by permission. www.Lockman.org

Scripture quotations marked (AMP) are taken from the Amplified® Bible, Copyright © 1954, 1958, 1962, 1964, 1965, 1987 by The Lockman Foundation. Used by permission. www.Lockman.org

Scripture quotations identified (Moffatt) are from The New Testament: A New Translation, copyright © 1964 by James Moffatt, published by Harper & Row, Inc. Used by permission.

Scripture quotations identified (J.B. Phillips) are from The New Testament in Modern English, translated by J. B. Phillips. © J. B. Phillips, 1958, 1960, 1972. Used by permission of Macmillan Publishing Co., Inc.

Scripture quotations identified as (MSG): Peterson, Eugene H. The Message: The Bible in Contemporary Language. Colorado Springs: NavPress, 2002, Used by permission. www.biblegateway.com

All emphasis in Scripture quotations is the author's.

Cover design by Rosie Moulton. rosie@el-modesigns.com

Artwork by Mark Murray. "Immersed in Love." Mark Murray is a part of New Earth Tribe. Used by permission.

ISBN: 978-1-621660-83-5

New Earth Tribe Publications © 2012
U.S.A. Edition - (Authorized by author Phil Mason)
Published by XP Publishing, a department of XP Ministries
P.O. Box 1017, Maricopa, AZ 85139
XPpublishing.com

About the Author

Phil Mason is married to Maria and has four adult children: three sons and a daughter. Together, Phil and Maria are the spiritual directors of New Earth Tribe: a spiritual community located in Byron Bay, Australia. New Earth Tribe was pioneered by Phil and Maria in 1998. Phil is also the director of the "Deep End School of the Supernatural" which is also located in Byron Bay. The school is a nine-month training program that equips and activates disciples of Christ in supernatural ministry. Phil completed a Bachelor of Theology at Flinders University in South Australia in 1991.

As the directors of New Earth Tribe, Phil and Maria planted the church on the foundation of the kingdom ministry of Jesus. They have sought to remain faithful to a divine mandate: not to allow their church to drift away from the call to build lives collectively upon the foundation of genuine intimacy with God and with one another in community. New Earth Tribe endeavours to be a community where everyone is committed to becoming a people of the heart. The principles and insights outlined in this book have been hammered out in the life of community. None of it is theory; it has all been comprehensively road-tested. Were it not for the twelve years of experience in building a community of people who welcome the supernatural ministry of Jesus to the heart, Phil would not have authority to address the issues contained in this series of books.

Phil is also the director of Christocentric Light, a ministry that takes teams into New Age festivals throughout Australia releasing demonstrations of the supernatural ministry of Christ. They are now seeing thousands of miracles in the New Age marketplace. Phil is also the director of the Byron Bay Healing Room and Byron Burn 24/7. To find out more about Phil and Maria and their ministry please visit the following websites.

www.newearthtribe.com
www.deependschool.com
www.philmason.org

Acknowledgements

To my wonderful wife: Maria. You are such a great inspiration to me and you definitely play a crucial role in keeping me on my heart journey. I have learnt so much from you in the 30 years we have journeyed together. Thanks for your patience in the countless hours I have spent writing this series of books in the midst of what is already a hectic schedule of pastoring, lecturing and traveling. You have supported and encouraged me all the way to continue this journey of writing to leave a legacy of our ministry together. Thank you so much for your enduring love and prophetic wisdom. I love you!

To my four adult children: Simon, Peter, Phoebe and Toby. You guys are so amazing and I love you all so much. Without you in my life I never would have known what it means to be a father. Thanks for all the kind words you have spoken over me.

To my spiritual community: New Earth Tribe of Byron Bay. Wow! How did I end up being so blessed to be a part of such a crazy, creative bunch of wild worshippers who love the supernatural ministry of Christ? I love each and every one of you who make up this glorious community and thank you a million times over for your constant love, support and encouragement.

To Stephen and Mara Klemich. Thank you so much for all of the support and encouragement you have given in the writing of this series of books. We are so grateful to the Father for bringing you both into our lives and we are looking forward to the years of journeying together in the Kingdom of God. Thanks both of you for your generous endorsements. You're all heart!

To Ken and Linda Helser: You have both been a secret source of inspiration to Maria and me in our journey. You have such a rich spiritual legacy in your family and you exemplify a family who have fought to pursue the journey of the heart. Thanks Ken for all of your encouragement to write these books and thanks for a delightful foreword. Stay on that eighteen inch journey!

Thanks also to Randy Clark, the father of the Toronto outpouring which has given rise to the Revival Alliance movement. Thanks for the very generous foreword to my book. Thanks to Wesley and Stacey Campbell. You are such kind hearted friends. Thanks Stacey for the endorsement and those late night conversations! Thanks to Charles and Anne Stock; we love you guys so much and are grateful to you for all of your encouragement. Thanks also to Peter McHugh, Bruce Lindley and Fini De Gersigny for your very kind endorsements. Thanks to my editorial team who have proof read my writings and for making great suggestions in how to improve these books. And finally, the biggest thanks and praise to Jesus. I hope this book glorifies You big time and advances Your kingdom by envisioning Your followers to get on board with the heart revolution. You deserve seven billion heartfelt worshippers!

THE SUPERNATURAL TRANSFORMATION SERIES

Contents

Endorsements

Phil Mason is brilliant! In this series of books on Supernatural Transformation, he gets to the heart of the matter. Relationships (with God
and people) are all about the heart. If our hearts are wounded and
jaded, every area of our lives are affected. But when we get to the
deeper places of God's heart, we find freedom and healing for our
own hearts. This series of books provides an exceptionally clear clarion
call to experience change that is real and lasting, not superficial and
transitory. I highly recommend them.

Stacey Campbell
Revival Now Ministries
Kelowna BC, Canada

Phil Mason lives and thinks outside the box! He does it with profound
integrity in the context of family and creative community. The book
you hold in your hand is many things. It's an antidote to superficial
pop spirituality. It's a beacon on the journey to the heart of reality. It's
more a compass than a map, orienting you toward the depths of your
own humanity and the heart of the One who made all that is. If you
are drawn to the mystery of authentic living, read on! Plunge into the
joy of the heart of God!

Charles Stock
Senior Pastor and River Guide
Life Center, Harrisburg, Pennsylvania

Phil Mason is an Australian revivalist and an apostolic father. He has pioneered a supernatural healing community in Byron Bay and taken the gospel of power from coast to coast as his teams impact the New Age fairs with signs, wonders, and miracles. This series of books will draw you into a deeper revelation of the finished work of the cross and your own supernatural role in the end time harvest.

Fini de Gersigny
Founder, Jubilee International Church
Sydney, Australia

Phil Mason is one of the greatest Christian thinkers in this generation. His unique teaching ability of combining great theology with practical Christian living results in this great resource – *The Supernatural Transformation Series*. I highly recommend that you buy these great books. They will be a point of reference for decades to come.

Bruce Lindley
Regional Director of Harvest International Ministries
Gold Coast, Australia

One of the great paradoxes of the Christian life is that we are becoming who we already are in Christ. Phil Mason in *The New Creation Miracle* has in a simple yet comprehensive way articulated how God's purpose is to unveil in the hearts of His people the life and righteousness of the redeemed. He helps the reader see the profound implications of the results achieved when Jesus identified with us at our worst so we could identify with Him at His best.

Peter McHugh
Senior Minister, Stairway Church Whitehorse
Melbourne, Australia

"Speaking from the heart," "heartfelt," the "heart of the matter," "being bottled up," and many other familiar sayings are not just sayings any more. The realization that we need to develop people's hearts and character is upon us. We are seeing the church return to Jesus' ministry to the heart for the development and transformation of people from the inside out. In our corporate consulting work, organizations have now adopted our "Smart with Heart" leadership and development programs globally. Phil's books are a read and re-read series that will stretch, strengthen, and lengthen your heart for bigger things.

Stephen Klemich
Founder of "HeartStyles" and "Achievement Concepts"
Sydney, Australia

Phil's series of books are a practical and biblically based exploration of Christ's ministry to the heart. Pursuing an understanding of the issues of the heart will bring you to a deeper intimacy with God. In seeking to recover the biblical knowledge and teaching on the heart, this series of books will lead you on a journey to reconciliation with the heart of God.

Mara Klemich, Ph.D.
Co-founder of "HeartStyles" and Consulting Psychologist
Sydney, Australia

Foreword
By Randy Clark

Phil Mason's new four volume series, *The Supernatural Transformation Series*, boldly endeavors to deepen the work of revival and renewal in the church. This series will take us back to the foundational issue of the supernatural miracle of regeneration and deepen our understanding of the experience of justification and sanctification as they relate to this miracle of regeneration. God has given us a brand new heart and this is a supernatural act of heaven invading earth.

Volume I: ***The Knowledge of the Heart*** is a strong biblical exploration of the importance the Bible places upon the heart. Phil gives us a thorough understanding of the meaning of "heart" in the Bible, and he calls the people of God to fully embrace the heart journey that Jesus intends each of His followers to recover. Jesus lives within what Phil identifies as the "intimacy paradigm." We are called to embrace this paradigm from the heart and allow it to revolutionize and transform our lives from the inside out. Intimacy is a journey of the heart.

Volume II: ***The New Creation Miracle*** focuses upon the issue of conversion and the reality that God has performed the miracle of giving us a brand new heart. Phil notes, "The new creation is the cornerstone and foundation of all Paul's theology. If Paul could communicate just one thing to believers it would be the revelation of the new creation." Phil emphasizes that this new creation event is an actual new "creation" of God; it is not just a theological fact but also an experiential reality. It is a supernatural reality, not just an abstract theological reality. In fact, the new creation miracle is the focal point of heaven invading earth.

Phil engages deeply with the subject of the finished work of Christ in this book. He asserts that the distinction between the finished work in our spirit and the unfinished work in our soul is part of the subtext of the New Testament. Phil focuses on how this revelation explains the paradox that calls us sanctified, yet we must pursue sanctification; we are cleansed but we must pursue cleansing. Phil's insights into the relationship between justification and sanctification are important in maintaining a clear biblical balance. The author also places a strong emphasis upon learning how to align ourselves with the fact of our co-crucifixion with Christ. Phil emphasizes that God cannot do this for us; we must develop the art of coming into alignment with the finished work of regeneration through the weapon of our will.

Volume III: *The Heart Journey* focuses on the New Testament concept of "entanglement." Phil identifies seven major arenas of entanglement revealed in the New Testament: the entanglement of Satan's lies, the entanglement of sin and selfishness, the entanglement of the tree of knowledge of good and evil (meaning entanglement in the law – the mind-set of external rules and regulations), the entanglement of worldly temptation, the entanglement of wounded and broken emotions, the entanglement of demonic infiltration, and the entanglement of physical biochemistry. This last sphere of entanglement explores the implications of living in a physical body that has been deeply corrupted by the fall.

Volume IV: *The Glory of God and Supernatural Transformation* focuses upon the theme of deep-level heart transformation explored through the lens of the ongoing supernatural kingdom ministry of Jesus to the hearts of His people. This book places particular emphasis upon Jesus' ministry of healing the brokenhearted, a theme that has been greatly neglected by the church. In seeking to deepen our understanding of this ministry, Phil gives us five keys to healing the brokenhearted. These are biblical revelation, the call to forgiveness and repentance, experiencing the glory of the Father's love, and discipleship. He follows up his emphasis upon healing the broken hearted with a similar emphasis upon the issue of demonization and the Christian, and the biblical ministry of demolishing demonic strongholds. Phil explores the biblical relationship between broken-heartedness, demonization, and the new creation.

Phil concludes the last book in his series by presenting a bold vision for the kind of supernatural freedom that Jesus intends to bring into the hearts of His people. He explores God's intention to bring many sons and daughters to glory and to fill our hearts with the glory of the Lord. This transformation from glory to glory can only be experienced as Christians receive the fullness of the kingdom ministry of Jesus. Phil emphasizes that this deep level of heart transformation is entirely supernatural and predicated upon the church entering into the fullness of the charismatic paradigm so that we can receive all that God is seeking to pour out upon his Church. The glory of the Lord can only cover the earth as Christians are fully awakened to the supernatural ministry of Jesus and as they step into the fullness of the new creation miracle.

It is Phil's desire that this series of books will lay a strong theological foundation for training God's people in the nature of New Testament heart ministry; a supernatural ministry that calls the church to focus on deeply transforming the hearts of God's people. This is not just through an abstract "positional righteousness," but through the experiential gift of righteousness. Not just through the experience of justification, but through the ongoing experience of the joy and freedom of sanctification. Phil also recaptures the emphasis of the early church that emphasized that the ministry of the Spirit—being filled with the Spirit—is intended to be part of the regeneration experience.

I believe Phil Mason's new four volume series, *The Supernatural Transformation Series*, is an important contribution to the present day theological discussion that is seeking to refocus our theology upon the Bible. This series allows the Bible to speak for itself, not allowing it to be interpreted through historical theological paradigms, whether they are Protestant, Roman Catholic, Orthodox, or even Pentecostal traditions. This is a read that will enlighten all of us. But more than that, it will challenge you to embrace the heart journey as you seek to live from the heart in pursuing a deeper intimacy in your relationship with God and with one another. It is time for a widespread heart revolution in the church!

Randy Clark
Global Awakening
Mechanicsburg, Pennsylvania
www.globalawakening.com

Foreword
By Ken Helser

It so happens that I was working on a book called *Living from the Heart* at the same time Phil was studying and putting together his early manuscripts on a book on the heart. Once while I was staying in his home, he gave me a copy and I nearly did not sleep the entire night because I was so engrossed in his material.

I am thrilled that Phil is finally getting these messages published. Why? Because when I first announced I was working on a book about the heart, more pastors than I could count confronted me with the question, "What exactly do you mean by the heart?" They had no clue and were so confused, which got me digging. Digging deep I asked, "Lord, what do You mean by the heart?"

Wow! That's about the same time I read Phil's material. He put it into words so simple that I got pumped and now I'm more pumped than ever. I could finally put in words what the "heart" meant not just to me but to God. Yeah! Thank you Phil, for digging out what God really means by the word "heart." May this series of books go all over the world, for the "heart of the matter" is what matters most to God.

At our ministry, A Place for the Heart, we've run a school for years now called *The Eighteen Inch Journey*. It has transformed the lives of young folks from all over the world, yet we are constantly asked, "What do you mean by calling it an eighteen inch journey?" We always answer, "Oh, that's the distance between your head and your heart." Still, without careful digging and revelation you cannot know what that means.

So, finally my good friend Phil Mason has poured not just his head, but also his whole heart into this series of books on the heart. I've read them and highly endorse him and his work, for every believer must make the *Eighteen Inch Journey* in order to live from the Spirit and not the head... and if you are not American, that's called the *45.7 Centimeter Journey*.

A wise man once said, "You cannot give what you haven't got any more than you can come back from where you haven't been." The reason I can read Phil Mason's messages on the heart and come alive from his revelation is not necessarily because he's brilliant, but because he's lived everything he's written. Nothing that Phil gives is second-hand information, but the overflow of living from the heart of God! Read Phil's work and you too will understand that you are reading a man's heart that has encountered the very heart of God first hand.

Ken Helser Ministries
A Place for the Heart
Sophia, North Carolina, USA
www.aplacefortheheart.org

Introduction

This book is the product of a spiritual journey that began thirty-three years ago. When I came to Christ in late 1979, God very graciously led me to a spiritual community on the East Coast of Australia where the pastor had a great passion for the Word of God. I found myself in an environment where the Word of God was honoured and the passion for spiritual revelation was contagious. I plunged myself into Bible study using all of the tools I could get my hands upon, soaking up hundreds of teachings from great Bible teachers all over the world and making many of my own discoveries in the Scriptures.

I was strongly attracted to a select handful of internationally recognised teachers, but there was one Bible expositor in particular who had a tremendous influence on my life. This teacher had an extraordinary Spirit of revelation upon him and I listened to many hundreds of hours of his teachings on cassette tape, which was the audio medium of the day. This man was a true new creation prophet who, to this day, has a greater grasp on many new creation realities than most of the teachers I have heard over the decades.

It was a great privilege to be given such a strong start in my walk as a follower of Jesus. As the decades have rolled by, I thank God for the foundation He laid in my life in those early years and the rich deposit of such powerful revelation that I received in the early 1980s. Of course, I have grown in a much greater depth of insight and wisdom since then. I have accumulated a much richer understanding of the miracle of the new creation since those early days. The glorious gospel truths contained in these pages are a distillation of a life of growing in an ever deepening love for the truth of God's word and the impact the Word of God is capable of bringing in our hearts as we are established in the truth.

The theme of this book, *The New Creation Miracle,* focuses on the heart of the New Testament believer. In contrast to the heart of the Old Testament believer, the heart of the man or woman who believes in Jesus has been transformed inwardly by a glorious miracle. A supernatural creative miracle has occurred at the core of the believer's heart. This miracle becomes the foundation for the comprehensive transformation that God intends to perform in the life of every follower of Jesus. The New Testament is a glorious revelation of the miracle that has occurred inside the hearts of those who believe in Jesus.

As we begin to awaken to the reality of this miracle that has already taken place, we begin to experience the power of the new creation. Faith precedes experience but experience must accompany faith! God seeks to bring every born again son or daughter to the "full assurance of faith" that they have been spiritually raised from the dead just as Jesus was physically raised from the dead. This miraculous operation of the Holy Spirit is the only foundation for change. Outside of this miracle we are left with nothing but self-effort and religious striving to try to emulate the heart of Jesus in our own strength.

In the Old Testament, God unveiled the heart of fallen man. He revealed that "The heart is deceitful above all things and desperately wicked; who can know it?" (Jeremiah 17:9). In the New Testament, God unveils the heart of the redeemed man. "Therefore, if anyone is in Christ, he is a new creation; old things have passed away; behold, all things have become new" (2 Corinthians 5:17). God intentionally juxtaposes the heart of the fallen man or woman with the heart of the redeemed man or woman.

Under the Old Covenant, the deeper God dredged up the contents of the heart, the more wickedness and sin was brought into the light. But in the New Covenant, the deeper God digs into the heart that has experienced this miraculous resurrection from the dead, the more He unveils the life and righteousness of the redeemed. He loves to call out the treasure of the new creation He has performed. The new birth is nothing short of a creative act of God. Paul said, "For we are His workmanship, ***created*** in Christ Jesus" (Ephesians 2:10). We are new creations because God has re-created us at the core of our being!

Resurrection life and power now characterizes the heart of the saint, whereas sin and death characterized the heart of the sinner. Everything must now be viewed through the revelatory prism of this new creation miracle! Without an ever-deepening revelation of the miraculous nature of the new creation, we will never comprehend the reality that God now relates to us as redeemed sons and daughters. He does not know us any longer "according to the flesh." Instead, He relates to us as beloved sons and daughters who are brand new on the inside. God no longer relates to us as sinners, but as saints!

Without this upgraded New Covenant knowledge of the heart we will continue to relate to ourselves as "desperately wicked." Indeed, this is the devil's master plan: to keep us locked into a perception of ourselves that characterized our life before we experienced the new creation miracle. How many Christians still relate to themselves as fallen sinners instead of redeemed saints? How many Christians still think of themselves as orphans instead of sons? How many of us be-have like orphans because we don't know who we are in Christ? If we are to partake of the mind of Christ, we need to be radically renewed in our thinking, not only about God, but also about ourselves.

God is bringing a revolution to the church. At the heart of this revolution is a shift in perspective. God is transforming the minds of His sons and daughters to such an extent that there is a generation of radical revolutionaries emerging who are becoming new creation prophets. There is a new generation of believers arising who have become gripped by this single revelation. You can distinguish them by one defining attribute: get them talking and they will begin to expound upon the miracle that has taken place in their heart. Paul was a forerunner. He was deeply committed to unveiling the heart of the New Testament believer. He was the ultimate new creation prophet!

This new creation miracle changes everything. It is the most powerful revolution that can ever impact a human being. Those who have experienced the rush and exhilaration of living in the resurrection power of this life-transforming miracle want to shout it from the rooftops! This miracle is the best thing that could ever happen to someone. It is not only "good news," it is the best news ever to be declared on our planet. How do you know when you have seen it the way God intends you to see it? You will become obsessed like Paul and the glory of God's grace will be all you want to talk about. I am somewhat cautious about teachers who move on to "more fertile fields of revelation" because it leaves me wondering if they have really seen the true nature of this incredible miracle.

I want to encourage you to come with me on a theological journey of deep spiritual revelation. Each chapter in this book is a building block of New Testament revelation. As the building blocks of revelation are put in place and interlocked, we come to a place of clear comprehension and depth of insight into all that God has done inside our heart. This revelation is utterly indispensible for the follower of Jesus. Every Christian ought to be so immersed in this stream of divine revelation that they become obsessed with the truths that constitute this new paradigm.

There are parts of this book that are slightly repetitive because we are looking at the same miracle from about a dozen different angles. There will be some overlap between chapters but I encourage you to see the repetition of the revelation as a cinematic landscape filmed from a multitude of unique camera angles. Every angle explores what

God has done in the human spirit and unpacks the implications for the ongoing transformation of our soul. We will be gazing into the matrix of creation itself to plumb the depths of God's supernatural handiwork in the comprehensive renewal of the human spirit.

There is no doubt that God wants this revelation to become clearer and clearer. The Holy Spirit is the Spirit of Wisdom and Revelation. He comes to unveil the finished work of Jesus on the cross as well as the invisible work of Jesus inside the hearts of those who have put their faith and trust in Him. As you read this book you will be cooperating with the Spirit of God who delights in unveiling the fullness of all that Jesus said and accomplished on earth.

We will never fully comprehend all that God has done. There is always room for growth in revelation and understanding. Paul prayed, "That your love may abound more and more in knowledge and depth of insight" (Philippians 1:9 NIV). The revelation of the new creation hinges upon a cluster of unique New Testament revelations that work together to build a deepening unveiling of the intensity and marvel of this miracle. It is not one single revelation but a combination of interlocking revelations. "The new wine is found in the cluster" (Isaiah 65:8).

Each singular revelation magnifies the other revelations until we are brought to a place of awe and amazement at the brilliance of the glory of God in His plan of redemption and salvation. I am in awe of the interlocking nature of these revelations. Each single revelation is like a piece of the jigsaw puzzle. But this jigsaw puzzle is unlike conventional puzzle pieces. These puzzle pieces are like fragments of light in a window to another world, and as the pieces are placed together and interlocked, they allow more and more light to stream into our understanding.

Just one or two pieces allow sufficient light to stream into our hearts to bring us to the place where we are blown away by the genius of God and His spectacular redemption of fallen human beings. But when all the pieces of this puzzle are interlocked with one another, it allows the radiance and splendour of the glory of heaven to illuminate us in such a way that we cannot live as we once lived. Paul lived in the light of the new creation miracle and He was utterly amazed and transported in rapture and ecstasy. Give him the microphone and he could talk all day and into the night!

Paul was a radical new creation prophet who was gifted with a capacity to articulate and communicate the full radiance of the gospel message. Everything he wrote was motivated by his singular desire to see every believer powerfully established in new creation truths. He desired that his own passion for the gospel might be replicated in the hearts of millions of delighted believers all over the world who could also communicate the wonders of God's amazing plan of salvation. As I wrote these chapters there were moments when my breath was taken away by the glory of who God is and of what He has done to redeem us. The way the Scriptures are woven together to unveil the tapestry of the new creation is truly awe inspiring and powerfully transformational. Jesus knew exactly why He had to endure the cross. It was for the joy that was set before Him in bringing many sons to glory.

It is our privilege as sons and daughters of God to unpack the gift of this divine revelation. God has given us, as human beings, a unique capacity to magnify His great glorious works. "Remember to magnify His work of which men have sung" (Job 36:24). The next verse says, "Everyone has seen these things, but only from a distance" (NLT). As believers, we have all contemplated the mystery of salvation but God wants us to employ all of our creative faculties to *magnify* this great work of salvation. The new birth is a creative act of God. It is hidden from the eyes of mankind, deep within the hearts of those who believe. But the Spirit who searches all things relentlessly seeks to display what God has done. Once we can see it, we can join Him in magnifying God's creative wisdom and power.

Introduction

The word "magnify" comes from the Latin word *magnus,* which means "great." To magnify something means to draw out its intrinsic magnificence. "Oh, magnify the Lord with me and let us exalt His name together" (Psalms 34:3). My prayer is that this book will greatly magnify God and His glorious miracle of the new creation. Paul excelled in magnifying the miracle of salvation, but his prayer was that God would raise up an army of millions of Spirit-filled disciples who could understand and proclaim the glory of this miracle.

I am personally persuaded that there is no greater work on earth than the creative workmanship of God unveiled through the hidden work of the new creation miracle. A physical healing is a glorious miracle but it is only temporal. These corruptible physical bodies will one day be replaced by a glorified body. I have seen countless physical miracles over more than three decades but all of them are eclipsed by the miracle of salvation performed within one human heart. In contrast to physical miracles, the new creation is an eternal work with eternal consequences. I hope you enjoy reading this book as much as I enjoyed the journey of writing it.

Phil Mason
Byron Bay,
New South Wales, Australia
April, 2012

Chapter One

Jesus: The Wonderful Counsellor

For unto us a Child is born, unto us a Son is given; and the government will be upon His shoulder. And His name will be called Wonderful Counsellor, Mighty God, Everlasting Father, Prince of Peace. (Isaiah 9:6)

In the first book in this series we sought to establish the fact that only God knows the heart. If this is true, then it is impossible for us to arrive at an accurate knowledge of the true condition of our heart apart from submitting our heart and mind to the Word of God. We have also seen that God alone searches the heart and mind. His eyes are upon our heart, and His desire is to totally heal and restore our heart by conforming it to the heart of His Beloved Son. "'For I know the plans I have for you,' declares the Lord, 'plans to prosper you and not to harm you, plans to give you hope and a future'" (Jeremiah 29:11 NIV).

As we turn our focus to the person and ministry of Christ, we discover that Jesus embodies the quintessential ministry of God to the human heart. In this prophet from Nazareth we behold the only man who holds the key to the heart. Jesus said, "All the churches shall know that I am He who searches the minds and hearts" (Revelation 2:23). He alone is the skillful Heart Surgeon who operates not on hearts of flesh and blood, but upon the hidden person of the heart.

ᵢ with the scalpel because, like His Father, He seeks
ᵢ our heart to prevent us from dying of a spiritual heart
᷄ doesn't operate, we shall surely die!

The Wonderful Counsellor

One of the prophetic names of Jesus in Scripture is "Wonderful Counsellor" (Isaiah 9:6 NIV). The Father gave the Son this glorious title because He is the only Person in the entire universe who is truly qualified to counsel humanity. The wisdom of His divine counsel causes the wisdom of man to appear as utter foolishness. Isaiah declared that the Lord "is wonderful in counsel and excellent in guidance" (Isaiah 28:29). The book of Psalms opens with this beatitude: "Blessed is the man who walks not in the counsel of the ungodly" (Psalm 1:1). There is godly counsel and there is ungodly counsel. God rebukes His people for receiving counsel from anyone but Himself. ""Woe to the rebellious children,' says the Lord, 'Who take counsel, but not of Me'" (Isaiah 30:1).

God's heart was grieved by the rebellion of His people when they turned to the ungodly for counsel. "They would have none of My counsel and despised all My reproof. Therefore they shall eat the fruit of their own way, and be filled to the full with their own fancies" (Proverbs 1:31).

The history of the people of God in the Old Testament overflows with tragic narratives that powerfully illustrate the dreadful consequences of rejecting the counsel of the Lord. The children of Israel "soon forgot His works; they did not wait for His counsel" (Psalm 106:13). "They rebelled against the words of God, and despised the counsel of the Most High" (Psalm 107:11). "They do not know the thoughts of the Lord, nor do they understand His counsel" (Micah 4:12). "For who has stood in the counsel of the Lord, and has perceived and heard His word? Who has marked His word and heard it?" (Jeremiah 23:18). Nevertheless, "The counsel of the Lord stands forever, the plans of His heart to all generations" (Psalm 33:11).

The phenomenon of the people of God "leaning on their own understanding" is by no means restricted to Old Testament times. Jesus stood outside the door of the church of Laodicea saying, "I counsel you to buy from Me gold refined in the fire, that you may be rich; and white garments, that you may be clothed, that the shame of your nakedness may not be revealed; and anoint your eyes with eye salve, that you may see" (Revelation 3:18). It is not clear who the Laodiceans were receiving their counsel from, but somehow they came to the conclusion that they were rich and in need of nothing. Whenever the people of God reject or ignore the counsel of the Lord, they inevitably lapse into a state of spiritual deception.

As we have already seen, Isaiah prophesied that one of the names of the coming Messiah would be "Wonderful Counsellor." He also declared that "The Spirit of the Lord shall rest upon Him, the Spirit of wisdom and understanding, the *Spirit of counsel* and might, the Spirit of knowledge and of the fear of the Lord" (Isaiah 11:2). Jesus was clothed with the Spirit of counsel and He astonished everyone who heard Him teach. The counsel of God revealed in Jesus' ministry simply cannot be surpassed. The depth of insight unveiled in the teachings of Christ cannot be transcended or supplemented in any way. "Who has known the mind of the Lord? Or who has been His counsellor?" (Romans 11:34 NIV).

If we presume to add to the counsel of Christ, it begs the question: have we ever really grasped who this man Jesus really is? The Apostle John tells us that Jesus "knew what people were really like. No one needed to tell him about human nature" (John 2:24-25 NLT). Jesus is the only authority on human nature because He sees humanity through the eyes of God. "Nothing in all creation is hidden from God's sight. Everything is uncovered and laid bare before the eyes of Him to whom we must give account" (Hebrews 4:13 NIV).

Jesus has a penetrating understanding of the human heart, which radically eclipses that of any other person. He knows exactly what our problem is, and He knows exactly how to remedy it. His teachings are infinitely relevant to the heart of our problem but, because of the dullness of our hearts, we do not perceive the absolute relevance of His words. Jesus gives answers to questions that we are not even asking. He is light years ahead of the human race; the world is still not ready for the answers that Christ has already given to the most burning issues that face humanity. The words of Christ are a mountain of gold, but the world passes them by as though they were a pile of dung.

When we begin to apprehend, through revelation, who Jesus Christ really is, we begin to perceive the applicability of His teachings to the plight of the human condition. Then we realise that there is only one true counselling ministry and one true counsellor: the Lord Jesus Christ. Jesus seeks to train His disciples to counsel others and to extend His ministry throughout the earth, but we dare not venture to assume that His words may be added to or improved upon. "Do not add to His words, or He will rebuke you and prove you a liar" (Proverbs 30:6 NIV).

Those who undertake to counsel one another in the body of Christ must always remember that the ministry of counselling is one of the many expressions of the Jesus' kingdom ministry. Jesus seeks to minister His counsel through us in the power of the Holy Spirit. "If anyone speaks, let him speak as the oracles of God. If anyone ministers, let him do it as with the ability which God supplies, that in all things God may be glorified through Jesus Christ" (1 Peter 4:11). The only counsel worth giving is the counsel of Christ, and He has entrusted His people as stewards of His wise and glorious counsel.

Biblical counsellors are pre-eminently ministers of the Word of God. Remember the words of Jeremiah, "Who has stood in the counsel of the Lord, and has perceived and heard His word? Who has marked His word and heard it?" (Jeremiah 23:18). Only those who have stood in the heavenly counsel of the Lord themselves and have proven it in their own lives are competent to counsel others. We cannot afford to neglect the hard work of studying the Scriptures and saturating ourselves in the mind of the Lord. In order to be qualified to counsel others, we must know the Lord and minister the heart and mind of the Lord to every person we counsel. Then as we counsel others, we will do it with the confidence that "It is not you who speaks, but the Spirit of your Father who speaks in you" (Matthew 10:20). Participating in the ministry of Christ is far richer than just learning His words for the purpose of declaring His words to others. That is a very one dimensional concept of the ministry of Christ.

The revelation of gift-based counselling opens up a new vista of ministry skills that bring the heart and mind of Christ to every person we work with. The Scriptures introduce us into a realm of outreach that utilises spiritual gifts for the application of deep spiritual ministry to others. Paul described the gift of the word of knowledge and the word of wisdom as expressions of the prophetic ministry of Christ. These spiritual gifts are designed to open up a dimension of Christian ministry that catapults us into the supernatural realm. Suddenly we are not relying upon our knowledge of the Word of God alone, instead we are relying upon Jesus, the Wonderful Counsellor, to step into the counselling situation and to create a whole new heavenly dimension that results in supernatural transformation.

The Christian who has saturated his or her mind in the Word of God, knows the heart of the Father, is empowered by the Holy Spirit, and has learnt to operate in the gifts of the Holy Spirit is far better equipped to counsel than someone who simply has the proper academic credentials. If we are correctly trained in the Scriptures, we will have a thorough working knowledge of the heart. Like Jesus, we will understand human nature and the absolute applicability of the Scriptures to the human predicament. The theological focus of biblical counsellors ought to be exactly the same as that which is preached and taught from the pulpit. Charles Spurgeon once said that preaching the Word is like taking a bottle of water, shaking it up and showering it over the congregation. In contrast, he likened the ministry of counselling to taking the same water and carefully pouring it into individual bottles.

Ministry to the Heart

We have seen from the Scriptures that Jesus Christ is the Wonderful Counsellor and that, from a biblical perspective, there is no such thing as a counselling ministry outside of the ministry of Christ. But now we must proceed to examine the specific nature of Christ's ministry. The most important point that needs to be made from the outset is that Jesus has a clearly defined supernatural ministry. This ministry was outlined before Jesus even came to the earth. In Isaiah 61, the eternal Son spoke through the prophet Isaiah about the nature of His future ministry.

> The Spirit of the Sovereign Lord is upon me, because the Lord has anointed me to preach good news to the poor. He has sent me to bind up the brokenhearted, to proclaim free-dom for the captives and release from darkness for the pris-oners, to proclaim the year of the Lord's favour and the day of vengeance of our God, to comfort all who mourn, and provide for those who grieve in Zion – to bestow on them a crown of beauty instead of ashes, the oil of gladness instead of mourning, and a garment of praise instead of a spirit of despair. (Isaiah 61:1-3 NIV)

This was Jesus' mission statement. It was His divine "job description." The first thing Jesus did after His forty-day fast in the desert was to visit the synagogue in Nazareth and publicly read this passage from the scroll of Isaiah (Luke 4:18-19). The Father had sent Him on a mission to perform a highly specific ministry on the earth. Jesus was in absolute perfect alignment with His assignment so that we on earth could be granted a beatific vision of the ministry of God to the human heart. The works that Jesus did were not His own but, as He frequently explained, they were the works of His Father.

> The very works that the Father has given me to finish, and which I am doing, testifies that the Father has sent me." (John 5:36 NIV)

> Do you not believe that I am in the Father, and the Father in Me? The words that I speak to you I do not speak on My own authority; but the Father who dwells in Me does the works. Believe Me that I am in the Father and the Father in Me, or else believe Me for the sake of the works themselves. (John 14:10-11)

Jesus did not have a self-styled ministry. He only did what He saw the Father doing. The words that He spoke and the works that He did were an accurate representation of the words and works of His Father. Jesus said, "My Father has been working until now, and I have been working" (John 5:17). The primary work of Jesus was to reveal the heart of His Heavenly Father. As an extension of this task, He sought to raise up a company of disciples who would perpetuate this specific ministry that had been given to Him from the Father. Immediately after Jesus highlighted the fact that the works that He had done attested to the fact that He was sent by God, He made this statement to His disciples: "Most assuredly, I say to you, he who believes in Me, the works that I do he will do also; and greater works than these he will do, because I go to My Father" (John 14:12).

The disciples were solemnly appointed to continue the ministry of Jesus. "As the Father has sent Me, I also send you" (John 20:21). There was no room for a self-styled ministry among the disciples of

Jesus, any more than there was room for a self-styled ministry in the life of Jesus Himself. If the disciples were to try to establish their own ministry style according to what seemed right to them, we could be sure that they would no longer accurately represent the ministry of Jesus. They would be advancing their own ministry agenda whilst the ministry of Jesus would be completely neglected.

This point needs to be made very clearly because the church has consistently sought to establish its own self-styled ministry. There is only one ministry and that is the ministry of Jesus. The church has been called to collectively steward that ministry by passing on the very words and works of Jesus. Jesus said, "I tell you the truth, the Son can do nothing by himself; He can do only what He sees His Father doing, because whatever the Father does the Son also does" (John 5:19 NIV).

The church is called to operate within this same ministry paradigm. Jesus could see the Father; He could do exactly what He saw His Father doing. Now that we have seen Jesus, we can do exactly what we see Jesus doing, because everything He does mirrors what the Father does. If we deviate from the ministry of Jesus we will no longer accurately represent the heart and mind of our Heavenly Father. This single biblical truth could start a ministry revolution if we could only see the distinction between the ministry that came forth from the Father and the humanistic ministry agendas that come forth from man.

The first and most distinctive feature of Jesus' ministry was His undivided focus upon the heart. "For the Lord does not see as man sees; man looks at the outward appearance but the Lord looks at the heart" (1 Samuel 16:7). Jesus always looked upon the heart. All of His teachings focused upon issues of the heart, and He systematically revealed the heart in everything He said and did. Simeon prophesied concerning Christ that through His ministry "the thoughts of many hearts will be revealed" (Luke 2:35 NIV).

Upon close inspection, everything Jesus said had a direct bearing on the condition of people's hearts. Jesus had no time for religious externalism. He cut right through every form of sanctimonious appearance and brought people in contact with their real heart issues. Consider for a moment the themes of the teachings of Christ. He spoke of love, mercy, compassion, forgiveness, sin, hardness of heart, repentance, righteousness, peace, joy, integrity, truthfulness, justice, honesty, faithfulness, honour, purity, and humility just to name a few. These are all profound heart issues. Similarly, all of Jesus' parables revealed truths concerning the hidden attitudes and motives of the heart. Every single word of Jesus cuts right to the heart!

It was part of the ministry of Jesus to expose the innermost purposes, attitudes, and motives of the heart in order to reveal the hidden factors that truly dictate our behaviour and actions. Often, we are completely out of touch with the real reasons why we do or say certain things until Jesus comes and reveals the hidden motives behind our words and actions. In Revelation 2:23, Jesus said, "I am He who searches the minds and hearts." It is an expression of God's great love and grace that He has no intention of leaving us in the dark. Rather, He desires to expose the hidden thoughts and motives of our heart in order to promote deeper repentance, to transform our attitudes and intentions, and to release us from our captivity to the merry-go-round of wounded responses.

While the unveiling of the heart may be extremely painful and sometimes quite humbling, it is the only path to true freedom. Because of the painfulness of this process, many Christians prefer to remain blissfully ignorant of the true condition of their heart. These Christians occupy themselves with a form of Christianity that functions exclusively on the level of externalism, intellectualism, functionality, and outward conformity to a set of religious rules and regulations.

But for Jesus, discipleship was exclusively a matter of the heart. He said, "A disciple is not above his teacher, nor a servant above his master. It is enough for a disciple that he be like his teacher, and a servant like his master" (Matthew 10:24-25). Jesus revealed that the objective of Christian discipleship was not to conform people to an outward code of religious behaviours, but to transform their hearts. Biblical change is always change from the inside out. Through this process of the inner transformation of the heart, we become like Christ. That is authentic Christian discipleship: to become like our Master. Jesus taught that this inner supernatural transformation is impossible apart from the supernatural operation of the Holy Spirit within us. On one occasion, Jesus had an encounter with a wealthy young man who appeared to have a heart for the things of God.

> A certain ruler asked him, "Good teacher, what must I do to inherit eternal life?" "Why do you call me good?" Jesus answered. "No one is good — except God alone. You know the commandments: 'Do not commit adultery, do not murder, do not steal, do not give false testimony, honour your father and mother.'" "All these I have kept since I was a boy," he said. When Jesus heard this, He said to him, "You still lack one thing. Sell everything you have and give to the poor, and you will have treasure in heaven. Then come, follow Me." When he heard this, he became very sad, because he was a man of great wealth. Jesus looked at him and said, "How hard it is for the rich to enter the kingdom of God! Indeed, it is easier for a camel to go through the eye of a needle than for a rich man to enter the kingdom of God." (Luke 18:18-25 NIV)

Jesus perceived that there was still one thing that held this man back from entering the kingdom of God, so He challenged this wealthy young man to repent and turn away from his idolatrous love of money and turn fully in his heart to God. After hearing this, His disciples said, "Who then can be saved?" They knew that the only thing that distinguished the rich young ruler from other people was that this man had money, whereas most people did not. But they also intuitively realised that the condition of men's hearts was basically the same. Everybody loved money and everybody was fundamentally greedy.

How then could greedy people be saved? How could the heart of a greedy man or woman be changed? Upon hearing the words of Jesus, they were faced with the impossibility of this kind of change. Jesus replied, "What is impossible with men is possible with God" (Luke 18:27). No amount of self-effort can change the basic nature of the human heart. "Can the Ethiopian change his skin or the leopard its spots? Neither can you do good who are accustomed to doing evil" (Jeremiah 13:23). Jesus taught that "Everyone who sins is a slave of sin" (John 8:34 NLT). We cannot be free from sin in our own strength. No amount of education or commitment to moral uprightness or decency will produce the fruit of righteousness. The answer, of course, is that we need a brand new heart. It takes a miracle!

As the "Wonderful Counsellor" and the "Skillful Heart Surgeon," Jesus knows exactly how to begin the work of transforming a broken and fallen human life. First, He counsels us to repent and turn to Him. If we hear His voice and come to Him by faith, we receive the gift of eternal life. Through the miracle of the new birth God establishes a beachhead of the Kingdom of Heaven inside the human heart. On this foundation He proceeds to begin the work of supernatural transformation from the inside out. In the words of King David, "He restores my soul" (Psalm 23:3). Through the new birth, the glory of heaven has invaded earth. In the words of John Peterson's famous hymn:

Heaven came down and glory filled my soul

When at the cross my Saviour made me whole.

My sins were washed away and my night was turned to day

When heaven came down and glory filled my soul.[1]

Through the prophet Ezekiel, Jesus counsels humanity, in all of its sinfulness and brokenness, to "Cast away from you all the transgressions which you have committed, and get yourselves *a new heart and a new spirit*" (Ezekiel 18:31). Jesus' remedy for the fallen condition of the human heart is repentance. Only this is the gateway to the gift of a brand new heart. In the next chapter we will begin to unpack the actual dynamics of the new heart and the new spirit that God places inside of every born again son and daughter. The new creation miracle is the foundation of supernatural transformation. It opens up a glorious destiny of deep heart transformation in which believers begin to transition from one degree of glory to another until we begin to look just like Jesus.

What does the Wonderful Counsellor say to a fallen world awash in sin and shame? ***"Get yourselves a new heart and a new spirit!"***

Chapter Two

A New Heart and a New Spirit

> I will give you a new heart and put a new spirit within you; I will take the heart of stone out of your flesh and give you a heart of flesh. I will put My Spirit within you and cause you to walk in My statutes, and you will keep My judgments and do them.
> (Ezekiel 36:26-27)

In the sixth century B.C., Ezekiel prophesied of a future time when God would give His people a brand new heart. If we look carefully at the prophecy of Ezekiel, we will see that there are two distinct elements to this New Covenant promise. The new heart and the new spirit are the result of the regenerating work of the Spirit inside of us, distinguished from the gift of the Spirit of Christ to us. According to Ezekiel, God gives us a new spirit but He also puts His own Spirit within us. Nevertheless, these two distinct elements are interrelated, because God's Holy Spirit cannot be supernaturally joined to an unregenerate human spirit. Your spirit, prior to the new birth, was comprehensively defiled by sin and rendered spiritually dead. Another way of expressing this is to say your spirit was alive to sin and dead to God.

The free gift of a brand new spirit and a brand new heart is prerequisite to the impartation of the gift of the Holy Spirit. Whilst this supernatural new creation takes place the very moment we put our faith in Christ, there are two separate elements to the new birth. One element is chronologically dependent upon the other, even though these twin miracles occur simultaneously. God cannot be united with sin, so He gave you a brand new spirit that is now supernaturally rendered dead to sin. Paul called this your "new self" who has been "created to be like God in true righteousness and holiness" (Ephesians 4:24 NIV). This is the new creation miracle.

Before Adam fell into sin, his human spirit was one hundred percent alive to God. Adam's spirit was also completely dead to sin, just as Jesus' spirit was four thousand years later when He walked upon the earth. But God warned Adam that if he were ever to disobey Him, he would instantaneously die. "But of the tree of the knowledge of good and evil you shall not eat, for in the day that you eat of it you shall surely die" (Genesis 2:17). Adam died spiritually in the split second he disobeyed God. His spirit was suddenly made alive to sin and dead to God. This new state of being spiritually dead appears to be a contradiction because, biologically, Adam lived for hundreds of years after the fall. But his spirit was now comprehensively dead in reference to God.

Through his own transgression, Adam passed from a state of being spiritually alive to a state of being spiritually dead. Sin always produces spiritual death because "the wages of sin is death" (Romans 6:23). Your human spirit is that part of you that is dead as a consequence of sin; this state of "death" is spoken of in biblical language in relationship to God and nothing else. For all intents and purposes, one can continue on their merry way in every other regard except that they are now completely "dead" in relation to God because they are "alive" to sin. The Bible teaches that every person born into the world is automatically dead to God because they were "in Adam" when he sinned against God. "Adam's sin brought death, so death spread to everyone, for everyone sinned" (Romans 5:12 NLT).

However, through the miracle of regeneration our human spirit passes from death to life. As John said, "We know that we have passed from death to life" (1 John 3:14). If you have received Christ, your spirit is now gloriously alive to God. Jesus Himself said, "Most assuredly, I say to you, he who hears My word and believes in Him who sent Me has everlasting life, and shall not come into judgment, but has passed from death into life" (John 5:24). Your spirit is that part of you which relates exclusively to God. Isaiah said, "Your iniquities have separated you from your God and your sins have hidden His face from you" (Isaiah 59:2).

Our human spirit is custom designed to engage with and respond to God. It is uniquely responsive to His voice. Peter taught that we are born again through the direct agency of the Word of God. "For you have been born again, not of perishable seed, but of imperishable, through the living and enduring word of God" (1 Peter 1:23 NIV).

How is our spirit brought back to life? The creative voice of God, which said, "Let there be light" (Genesis 1:1), speaks over our dead human spirit. Like the voice of Jesus calling Lazarus forth from the tomb, so God speaks His creative Word and our spirit instantaneously passes from death to life in the twinkling of an eye. Jesus said, "Most assuredly, I say to you, the hour is coming, and now is when the dead will hear the voice of the Son of God; and those who hear will live" (John 5:25).

The difference between a dead human spirit and a spirit which has been made alive to God is so vast that it is like describing two different worlds. The best analogy I can come up with is the difference between a super massive star and a black hole. A stellar mass shines with unimaginable intensity and luminosity. It is as though a sun is a living furnace of energy and radiation that shines forth in every direction, simultaneously giving light and life to everything. The focus of a sun is outward as it radiates great quantities of energy from itself. In contrast, a black hole is a region of space from which nothing can escape, not even light. It is a deep and powerful gravitation vortex that sucks everything into itself.

A person who is bound by sin functions selfishly, like a black hole. They are self-centred and everything becomes about them as they effectively deify themselves and their own will as supreme and absolute. Self-interest dominates all of their decisions and choices because self is well and truly enthroned. But a person who has been made alive to God begins to radiate love because their spirit is now in Christ, and Christ, who is our life, shines forth radiantly in the glory of His great love. Paul said that those who are spiritually alive "shine like stars in the universe" (Philippians 2:15 NIV).

I once heard a preacher describe an incredible prophetic experience where he was carried away in the Spirit to the Garden of Eden to behold Adam before the fall. Disoriented, this person thought he was having an encounter with the King of Glory, but soon came to realise that it was a vision of Adam in his pristine glorified state. He described a being who glowed with an incredible beauty and radiance and even his footsteps carried an intense weight of glory. Seeing Adam before he fell into sin shook this man to his core as he suddenly realised just how far we have all fallen into sin and just how far we have fallen short of the glory of God. As the preacher told the story, I was drawn into a sense of the gravity of the experience and felt a sense of great awe overshadow me as I contemplated the majesty of this glorious being before the tragedy of his descent into sin and death.

I once heard another preacher speculate that Adam's human spirit, in union with the Spirit of God before the fall, was so great that he wore his spirit on the outside of his body as well as inside. While it is purely speculative, it does make sense because Adam's pristine spirit would have been so radiant in its unfettered state that it would have glowed and emanated beyond the parameters of his body and soul. Paul described Jesus as the "last Adam." He said, "So it is written:

'The first man Adam became a living being; the last Adam, a life-giving spirit'" (1 Corinthians 15:44-45 NIV).

Of course, Jesus was divine and Adam was not, but nevertheless, Adam must have been an exceedingly glorious being before he fell into sin. The connection between the "first Adam" and the "last Adam" is is clear: both of these beings radiated the glory of God on the earth. Jesus radiated the glory of God in an innate sense, because He was God manifested in flesh and blood. Adam radiated the glory in a secondary sense in that he was reflecting the glory of Christ. When Jesus was on earth, His spirit extended beyond the parameters of His physical being as He emanated an atmosphere of heaven and supernatural power. Similarly, Adam would have carried the presence of the glory in a way that also manifested an atmosphere that expressed all of the virtues of the divine nature. Human beings have been uniquely created to be the dwelling place of God on earth.

Imagine the very moment that Adam sinned: his unblemished spirit had been gloriously alive in God and radiated the glory of God with such majesty that someone might have mistaken him for a divine being. Yet, in a moment, his spirit was suddenly snuffed out as its polarity was mysteriously reversed and it instantaneously atrophied into a state of blackness and inward focus. One moment the light was switched on brightly and the next it was gone like a sudden collapsed star. One theory of the origin of black holes is that they were once massive stars that collapsed in upon themselves. It is hard to imagine such a catastrophic reversal from a glorious stellar object that radiated such extraordinary energy to a hyper-dense mass that now sucks everything into itself. But that is a graphic picture of the fate of Adam's human spirit as it was plunged from light into darkness and life into death.

Conversely, when a person believes in Jesus and is thrust from darkness and death into light, it would be like watching a black hole undergoing a complete polarity reversal and springing spontaneously into life. Suddenly there is an entirely new reality of light and life as the spirit springs spontaneously to life and begins to radiate energy outwardly for the first time in its existence. This is what would be seen from heaven's perspective as all over the earth people give their lives to Jesus. New lights are springing up everywhere as the "Father of lights" receives His newborn sons and daughters into His everlasting arms of love. All of a sudden people spring into life and new stars are born that have the potential to shine with unimaginable glory like Adam and even greater.

Your new spirit has been perfected in every way. The new nature of your human spirit is no longer a sin nature. It is righteous and holy, just like the human spirit of Jesus when He walked the earth. In fact, God has restored your human spirit to the pristine condition of Adam and Eve's spirits before they fell into sin. This is an extraordinary creative miracle wrought by the creative power of God. Through this miracle we have been spiritually raised from the dead and we are now gloriously alive to God.

Do you remember what God said about the human heart in the Old Testament? He said, "The heart is deceitful above all things and desperately wicked; who can know it?" (Jeremiah 17:9). The miracle is that this verse cannot be used anymore in reference to the born again believer. It is no longer true of those who are in Christ Jesus. We who have received Jesus Christ as our Saviour have been given a completely new spirit and a brand new heart. But we do not know ourselves yet. Paul said, "If anyone thinks that he knows anything, he knows nothing yet as he ought to know" (1 Corinthians 8:2). Paul said that this side of heaven all our knowledge is merely partial. "For we know in part and we prophesy in part. For now we see in a mirror, dimly, but then face to face. Now I know in part, but then I shall know just as I also am known" (1 Corinthians 13:9,12). We are all in the midst of an unfolding, yet imperfect knowledge of who we are in Christ.

The Revival of the Human Spirit

Just as Ezekiel prophesied concerning the regeneration of the human spirit, so also did Isaiah. He declared prophetically that God would revive (bring back to life) the human spirit, actually bringing it back from the dead. "For thus says the High and Lofty One who inhabits eternity, whose name is Holy: 'I dwell in the high and holy place with him who has a contrite and humble spirit, to revive the spirit of the humble and to revive the heart of the contrite ones'" (Isaiah 57:15). The humble and contrite ones are those who have responded to the gospel call to repentance. Repentance has always been the doorway into the Kingdom of God. The Lord promised through Isaiah that He would fully revive those who believed and repented of their sins by turning to God. The Hebrew word for "revive" is *chayah*, and it means *to quicken, to give life or to restore to life*. The focal point of this glorious revival from the dead is the human spirit.

But there is even more to this glorious new creation, because this gift of new life heralds the advent of an entirely new nature. Peter revealed that the new birth paves the way for believers to "participate in the divine nature" (2 Peter 1:4 NIV) as a consequence of the indwelling of the Spirit of Christ. It is important to note that the regenerative work of the Spirit in your human spirit does not make your new nature divine, but it does create a union between the nature of Christ and our revived spirit. This is the mystery of our mystical union with Christ. He is divine, therefore we get to partake of His divine nature. We never become divine but we become carriers of, and participants in the divine nature of Christ.

Paul said, "We have this treasure in earthen vessels that the excellence of the power may be of God and not of us" (2 Corinthians 4:7). Through the new birth this divine nature of Christ is welded to your human spirit. "He who is joined to the Lord is one spirit with Him" (1 Corinthians 6:17).

Your spirit and the Spirit of God are now inseparably joined together. Paul said, "If Christ is in you ... your spirit is alive because of righteousness" (Romans 8:10 NIV). This is a headline verse! Paul revealed that the focal point of the new birth is the human spirit. He spoke a lot about the human spirit because he recognised that we are spirit beings, just as God is a spirit being. Jesus said, "God is spirit" (John 4:24) and because we are made in the very image and likeness of God, we are also spirit.

This is important because we need to see that the gift of the "new heart" prophesied by Ezekiel has two aspects. We not only receive a new heart and a new nature, but the heart of Christ and His divine nature is also imparted to us. During the course of His ministry, Jesus promised His disciples that the time would come when He would mysteriously live inside of them. "In that day you will know that I am in My Father and you in Me, and *I in you*" (John 14:20 NASB). When Christ comes to live in our hearts through the new birth, we actually receive the free gift of the heart of Christ Himself.

The new heart that God has given those who have turned to Him is actually the heart of Christ united with our brand new spirit. It is through this miracle that we have become partakers of the divine nature. The old heart of stone has now been replaced by the new heart of Christ in us. The New Testament revelation of "Christ in you" (Colossians 1:27) is God's answer to the old heart of stone. However, this new heart of Christ has been planted inside of our heart in seed form. John proclaimed that God's "***seed remains***" inside the heart of every believer who has been born of God (1 John 3:9). It is as though we have a new heart embedded within our own heart. If the biblical idea of the heart consists of everything that constitutes our interior life, then it is true that we have a "heart within a heart." We have the heart of Christ in us but we still have the legacy of the old heart that lingers on. If we are going to begin this heart journey of supernatural transformation, we have to take seriously the issues of the heart that hinder our spiritual growth, otherwise we will completely stagnate in our spiritual journey.

The New Testament paradigm consists of the revelation of the heart of Christ indwelling the heart of the believer. Nowhere do the New Testament writers indicate that the miracle of the new birth results in an instantaneously perfect heart. Clearly there are all sorts of challenges, struggles, and difficulties that beset the believer, because our hearts are transformed incrementally as we volitionally step into a progressive conformity to the image of Christ. There are numerous factors at work in the battle to be conformed to the perfect, loving heart of Christ.

A major key to living in the power of the new creation is in learning to embrace the revelation that we are no longer defined by what we once were when we lived exclusively for ourselves. God is continually calling out the treasure in our lives, and He no longer knows us according to the flesh.

> For the love of Christ compels us, because we judge thus: that if One died for all, then all died; and He died for all, that those who live should live no longer for themselves, but for Him who died for them and rose again. Therefore, from now on, we regard no one according to the flesh. Therefore, if anyone is in Christ, he is a new creation; old things have passed away; behold, all things have become new. (2 Corinthians 5:14-17)

If God no longer knows us according to our old self-centred state of existence, but sees us as glorious new creations, should we not also cease from knowing ourselves according to who we were before Christ entered our hearts? Paul gave his readers dozens of keys to live in the reality of the new creation. However, all of these keys only work if we believe that we are now who God says we are. God begins His work of supernatural transformation with an explosion of new creation glory. He launches us into a lifestyle of ever increasing victory over sin, darkness, and brokenness. He gets us off to a fresh start by making us brand new on the inside. We fight from a position of victory based upon the new creation miracle. We never engage in warfare against the world, the flesh, and the devil from a place of defeat because God has already won a decisive victory within us through the new birth. If only we could gain this prophetic perspective in our warfare, we would understand that we have already been seated with Christ in heaven far above principalities and powers. He has already given us dominion and power over sin because Christ is in us!

In the next chapter we will begin to zoom in on the dynamics of the new creation so that the miracle that God has already performed within our hearts can come into clear focus. Only then will we be powerfully equipped to recognise who we are in Christ and be able to put on Christ in such a way that we begin to appropriate the fullness of this transformational power.

Chapter Three

The Circumcision of the Heart

In the previous chapter we explored the theme of the gift of the new heart. We saw that Ezekiel prophesied that God would put a new heart in those who believe and that this promise was fulfilled in the era of the New Covenant. We established that Christ now lives in our heart but we also recognised, through the writings of Paul, that the legacy of the old life still lingers within our hearts as well. The totality of my heart is thus a mixture of old and new. The old is continually passing away and the new is continually in the ascendency as long as I continue to embrace and appropriate by faith the reality that I am a glorious new creation. In this chapter I want to develop a clear theological paradigm that will cut through any remaining confusion by giving you a deeper insight into the actual mechanics of the new creation miracle. Paul said,

> From now on, we regard no one according to the flesh. Therefore, if anyone is in Christ, he is a new creation; old things have passed away; behold, all things have become new. All this newness of life is from God, who has reconciled us to Himself through Jesus Christ, and has given us the ministry of reconciliation, that is, that God was in Christ reconciling the world to Himself, not imputing their trespasses to them,

47

and has committed to us the word of reconciliation. Now then, we are ambassadors for Christ, as though God were pleading through us: we implore you on Christ's behalf, be reconciled to God. For He made Him who knew no sin to be sin for us, that we might become the righteousness of God in Him. (2 Corinthians 5:16-21 NKJV/NLT)

Paul's theology of the new creation is the product of extraordinary divine revelation. The new creation is the cornerstone and foundation of all Paul's theology. If Paul could communicate just one thing to believers, it would be the revelation of the new creation. This new creation is an actual fact. It is not something which God merely regards to be theoretically true because we believe. It is an actual state which God has miraculously wrought in our hearts and is therefore the result of a supernatural operation upon our heart. God has cut something away from inside our heart. He has divided our heart with His mighty sword and created an actual separation within us between the old and the new. The biblical language for this supernatural operation is the "circumcision of the heart."

In the Old Testament, God ordained the circumcision of every male child as a sign of their participation in the Abrahamic Covenant. This sign preceded the establishment of the Mosaic Covenant at Mount Sinai but it was also carried on as a sign of participation in the Mosaic Covenant.

> When Abram was ninety-nine years old, the Lord appeared to Abram and said to him, "I am Almighty God; walk before Me and be blameless. And I will make My covenant between Me and you, and will multiply you exceedingly." Then Abram fell on his face, and God talked with him, saying: "As for Me, behold, My covenant is with you, and you shall be a father of many nations. No longer shall your name be called Abram, but your name shall be Abraham; for I have made you a father of many nations. And I will establish My

covenant between Me and you and your descendants after you in their generations, for an everlasting covenant, to be God to you and your descendants after you. This is My covenant which you shall keep, between Me and you and your descendants after you: Every male child among you shall be circumcised; and you shall be circumcised in the flesh of your foreskins, and it shall be a sign of the covenant between Me and you. He who is eight days old among you shall be circumcised, every male child in your generations. And the uncircumcised male child, who is not circumcised in the flesh of his foreskin, that person shall be cut off from his people; he has broken My covenant." (Genesis 17:1-5, 7, 10- 12, 14)

Circumcision of the flesh pointed prophetically toward a different kind of circumcision. In the book of Deuteronomy, God began to speak to His people about their need to be circumcised in their hearts. At first, He gave it as a command: "Therefore circumcise the foreskin of your heart, and be stiff-necked no longer" (Deuteronomy 10:16). Later in Deuteronomy, Moses promised, "The Lord your God will circumcise your heart and the heart of your descendants, to love the Lord your God with all your heart and with all your soul that you may live" (Deuteronomy 30:6).

This promise in Deuteronomy pointed toward a prophetic fulfillment of the rite of physical circumcision. In other words, physical circumcision, the cutting away of the foreskin of every male, pointed toward the New Covenant established by Jesus when God would cut away the sinful nature inside the hearts of His people, both men and women.

Once the New Covenant was established through the shedding of Christ's blood on the cross, the definition of a true Israelite shifted from one who had the outward sign of circumcision in the flesh to one who was spiritually circumcised in their heart. Paul found it necessary to redefine the very essence of what it meant to be Jewish. "For he is not a Jew who is one outwardly, nor is circumcision that which is outward in the flesh; but he is a Jew who is one inwardly; and circumcision is that of the heart, in the Spirit, not in the letter; whose praise is not from men but from God" (Romans 2:28-29).

Being a Jew was once defined exclusively by the ability to trace family genealogy back to their father Abraham. But the New Covenant shifted the basis from a physical genealogy and physical circumcision to a spiritual genealogy (all who have the faith of Abraham in their hearts) and a spiritual circumcision through the new birth. Those who have true faith in their hearts become the spiritual sons and daughters of Abraham. That is why Paul now called the church the "Israel of God."

> For in Christ Jesus neither circumcision nor uncircumcision avails anything, but a new creation. Peace and mercy to all who follow this rule, even to the Israel of God. (Galatians 6:15-16)

Paul actually redefined Israel. "For not all who are descended from Israel are Israel. Nor because they are his descendants are they all Abraham's children. In other words, it is not the natural children who are God's children, but it is the children of the promise who are regarded as Abraham's offspring" (Romans 9:6-8 NIV). The promise was the free gift of righteousness to those who share in the faith of Abraham. Physical circumcision has now been abolished through the establishment of a New Covenant. The prophetic sign has now been fulfilled through the cutting away of the sinful nature within the hearts of those who believe.

> When you came to Christ, you were "circumcised," but not by a physical procedure. It was a spiritual procedure — the cutting away of your sinful nature. For you were buried with Christ when you were baptized! And with him you were raised to a new life because you trusted the mighty power

of God, who raised Christ from the dead. You were dead because of your sins and because your sinful nature was not yet cut away. Then God made you alive with Christ. He forgave all our sins. He cancelled the record that contained the charges against us. He took it and destroyed it by nailing it to Christ's cross. In this way, God disarmed the evil rulers and authorities. He shamed them publicly by his victory over them on the cross of Christ. (Colossians 2:11-15 NLT)

In light of the new creation and the miracle of spiritual rebirth, Paul could now say, "For we are the circumcision, who worship God in the Spirit, rejoice in Christ Jesus, and have no confidence in the flesh" (Philippians 3:3). The New Living Translation makes this passage even clearer: "Watch out for those dogs, those wicked men and their evil deeds, *those mutilators* who say you must be circumcised to be saved. For we who worship God in the Spirit are the only ones who are truly circumcised. We put no confidence in human effort. Instead, we boast about what Christ Jesus has done for us" (Philippians 3:2-3 NLT). This circumcision of the heart has been performed surgically upon our hearts through the action of the Word of God. "For you have been born again, not of perishable seed, but of imperishable, through the living and enduring word of God" (1 Peter 1:23 NIV).

Jesus: The Skillful Heart Surgeon

The writer to the Hebrews explains exactly how this cutting away of the sinful nature takes place within our heart. "For the word of God is living and powerful, and sharper than any two-edged sword, piercing even to the division of soul and spirit, and of joints and marrow, and is a discerner of the thoughts and intents of the heart" (Hebrews 4:12). The Message Bible says, "His powerful Word is sharp as a surgeon's scalpel, cutting through everything" (Hebrews 4:12).

This is not a metaphorical cutting away! It is an actual cutting away of the sinful nature from the human spirit. Prior to this cutting away, the human spirit was comprehensively defiled by sin. It was even subject to demonic infiltration as it had no means of protection against the invasion of demonic influence. Before salvation the human spirit was dead, and death is the dominion of Satan and the demonic realm. The "wages of sin is death!" Death had contaminated and defiled our spirit and we were rendered dead to God through sin. Paul said you "were dead in trespasses and sins" (Ephesians 2:1).

The sharp, two-edged sword that proceeds out of the mouth of Jesus cuts away the sinful nature, relegating it exclusively to the yet un-renewed regions of the soul. Through the supernatural laser surgery of the Word, God created a clear line of demarcation between the un-renewed soul and the renewed human spirit, which has been made comprehensively righteous through the miracle of regeneration. God carves out a sanctuary for Himself right in the very centre of our heart! Let's return to the passage in Colossians and examine exactly what Paul tells us that God has surgically removed. "In Him you were also circumcised with the circumcision made without hands, by putting off the body of the sins of the flesh, by the circumcision of Christ" (Colossians 2:11). This same verse in the Amplified Bible reads, "In Him also you were circumcised with a circumcision not made with hands, but in a [spiritual] circumcision [performed by] Christ by stripping off the body of the flesh [the whole corrupt, carnal nature with its passions and lusts]." That is why Paul can now say, "You are not in the flesh but in the Spirit, if indeed the Spirit of God dwells in you" (Romans 8:9).

This verse in Colossians is clearly linked in Paul's thinking to Romans 6:6 where he uses a very similar phrase: "Knowing this, that our old man was crucified with Him; that the body of sin might be done away with; that we should no longer be slaves of sin." In Romans, Paul uses the phrase "the body of sin" whereas in Colossians he uses the phrase "the body of the sins of the flesh." There can be little doubt that he has the same thought in mind. The Colossian passage sheds light on the Romans passage because the term "body of sin" in

Romans 6:6 is somewhat ambiguous. The Colossian passage clarifies that the entire "body of the sins of the flesh" has been cut away through a supernatural circumcision. This means that we no longer have a sin nature at the very core of our being! Our sin nature has actually been eradicated or surgically removed.

The radical idea that the sin nature has been removed from the believer is called *eradicationism*. This term implys that the sin nature has been comprehensively eradicated from the life of the believer. Eradicationism is a very dangerous theology when it is not presented in the context of the full counsel of God. Because of its perfectionist implications, it can actually become a new form of legalism if Bible teachers are not extremely careful in the way they present this doctrine. Just to put things into historical context, there was a time in church history when the eradicationist teaching became quite popular. Eradicationism was a part of John Wesley's perfectionist theology in the 1700s; it eventually become a part of the theological fabric of the Holiness Movement. John Wesley wrote a booklet called *A Plain Account of Christian Perfection* in which he developed his doctrine of "entire sanctification." Wesley taught a kind of eradicationism without actually using the word itself. He preferred the word "extirpation," which essentially means the same thing. Extirpation means "to be destroyed or pulled up by the roots."

The biblical basis for the concept of the complete eradication of the old sin nature is derived from Colossians 2:11 and Romans 6:6, which says: "Knowing this: that our old man was crucified with Him, that the body of sin might be done away with." Another translation reads "destroyed." The doctrine of eradicationism hinges largely upon an interpretation of the term "done away with." The Greek word is *katargeo* and it has a range of meanings. Essentially, it means to "be destroyed, rendered useless, made of no effect, or to be abolished." *Katargeo* is used in Hebrews 2:14, "That through death He might *destroy* him who had the power of death, that is, the devil."

Paul taught that the work of the cross has comprehensively eradicated the old sinful nature. The fact that God has given us an entirely new nature that is righteous, holy, and free from sin supports this idea. When Romans 6:6 is linked to Colossians 2:11, it is evident that the old sin nature has quite literally been stripped away through the power of the cross. It no longer has the power over us that it once had. Unless, of course, we do not understand what Paul is really teaching.

There is further evidence in New Testament theology to indicate that this is the new state of all born again believers. John said, "Whoever has been born of God does not sin, for His seed remains in him; and he cannot sin, because he has been born of God" (1 John 3:9). The new nature of the believer cannot sin because it is holy and righteous. Oddly, in the same epistle John says, "If we say that we have no sin, we deceive ourselves, and the truth is not in us" (1 John 1:8). How do we reconcile these two ideas? John clearly acknowledged the ongoing struggle with sin and temptation in the life of every Christian. "My dear children, I write this to you so that you will not sin. But if anybody does sin, we have One who speaks to the Father in our defence; Jesus Christ, the Righteous One" (1 John 2:1 NIV). John taught the necessity for all believers to purify themselves from sin. "Everyone who has this hope in Him purifies himself, just as He is pure" (1 John 3:3).

John desired to see every believer delivered comprehensively from sin. Therefore, he placed his theological emphasis upon the believer learning to abide in Christ. "And now, little children, abide in Him." (1 John 2:28). "You know that He was manifested to take away our sins, and in Him there is no sin. Whoever abides in Him does not sin." (1 John 3:6). For John, the answer lies in the teaching of Christ when Jesus said, "Abide in Me, and I in you. As the branch cannot bear fruit of itself, unless it abides in the vine, neither can you, unless you abide in Me. I am the vine, you are the branches. He who abides in Me, and I in him, bears much fruit; for without Me you can do nothing" (John 15:4-5). John understood that there is a choice in this issue of abiding. Jesus said, "*If* you abide in Me..." (John 15:7).

Every believer knows the challenge of learning how to walk in obedience. John's theology of abiding in Christ parallels Paul's theology of walking in the Spirit. These are merely two ways of saying the same thing. Both John and Paul state the reality of the eradication of the sin nature yet their pastoral ministry focused on training believers how to walk in obedience and live according to the reality of what God has already done inside our hearts. The circumcision of the heart is a cutting away of all that is old from all that has been made brand new. The radicalism of Paul and John's new creation theology is deliberately designed to shock us into the reality of the finished work of Christ on the cross.

Your New Nature of Worship

In the moment your heart was supernaturally circumcised, your true inner nature was miraculously transformed. You passed from being a sinner to becoming a saint by nature. Because God removed your sin nature from your spirit, you are no longer a professional sinner. You were stripped of your enjoyment of sin because the Holy Spirit has now been fused to your spirit. Your new nature loves righteousness and hates sin. And your new nature is turned fully toward God in prayer and worship. You became a worshipper by nature at the new birth. If you are not growing in your life as an intimate worshipper, it simply means that you are not exercising or living out of your new nature in Christ. In the words of Bono from U2 in their outstanding worship song, "Magnificent:"

I was born, I was born to sing to You.

I didn't have a choice but to lift You up

And sing whatever song You wanted me to.

I give you back my voice from the womb.

My first cry, it was a joyful noise!

Justified till we die, You and I will magnify The Magnificent.[2]

Paul said, "For we are the circumcision, who worship God in the Spirit" (Philippians 3:3). The New Living Translation says, "For we who worship God in the Spirit are the only ones who are truly circumcised" (Philippians 3:2-3 NLT). The more we exercise this new worshipping nature the more we learn to live as a new creation. Worship is what new creations do! Jesus said, "God is spirit, and those who worship Him must worship in spirit and truth" (John 4:24). We exercise our spirit by worshipping God on the wings of the Spirit. Because our heart has been circumcised and we have a new worshipping nature, we engage in spirit to spirit communion with the Father. Prayer and worship has become the chief activity of your spirit. God even gives your spirit a new prayer language! Paul said, "For if I pray in a tongue, my spirit prays, but my understanding is unfruitful. What is the conclusion then? I will pray with the spirit, and I will also pray with the understanding. I will sing with the spirit, and I will also sing with the understanding" (1 Corinthians 14:14-15).

There is a huge party going on inside your spirit. *Praise and worship is the soundtrack of the new creation.* When the prodigal son came to his senses, he turned back to his Father's house. I want to draw your attention to what the Father said: "'Bring out the best robe and put it on him, and put a ring on his hand and sandals on his feet. And bring the fatted calf here and kill it, and let us eat and be merry; for this my son was dead and is alive again; he was lost and is found.' And they began to be merry. Now his older son was in the field. And as he came and drew near to the house, he heard music and dancing" (Luke 15:22-25).

The Father's house is now inside your spirit! Jesus said, "If anyone loves Me, he will keep My word; and My Father will love him, and We will come to him and make Our home with him" (John 14:23). There is a full-scale worship festival going on inside of you. The Greek word for "merry" is *euphraino* from which we derive the English word euphoria. It is variously translated as "rejoicing" or "celebrating." As you enter your spirit man, you are like the elder brother drawing near to the party in the Father's house. At first it sounds foreign and unfamiliar but as you become acclimatized, you realise this is the permanent atmosphere in the Father's house. The Amplified Bible says, "Let us revel and feast and be happy and make merry." The Wuest Translation says that the elder brother "drew near the house and heard music played by a number of musicians in concert, and the sound of people dancing a circular dance on the lawn" (Luke 15:25).

Jesus instructs you to go into your inner room. He said, "But you, when you pray, *go into your inner room*, close your door and pray to your Father who is in secret, and your Father who sees what is done in secret will reward you" (Matthew 6:6 NASB). There is a lot of glory inside the Father's secret place. The Father sings over us, and Jesus sings to the Father. The Father is continuously celebrating your sonship and your redemption. "The Lord your God in your midst, the Mighty One, will save; He will rejoice over you with gladness, He will quiet you with His love, He will rejoice over you with singing" (Zephaniah 3:17). Jesus also lives inside of you. He says to the Father, "I will declare Your name to My brethren; in the midst of the assembly I will sing praise to You" (Hebrews 2:12).

Did you know that there is an untapped reservoir of euphoric celebration going on inside your spirit? There is a lot of glory inside your spirit and this resident glory of God has the capacity to usher you into a state of deep ecstasy and bliss. "Now to Him who is able to keep you without stumbling or slipping or falling and to present you unblemished (blameless and faultless) before the presence of His glory in triumphant joy and exultation (with unspeakable, ecstatic delight)" (Jude 24 Amp.). One of the greatest ways we can exercise our renewed spirit is by worshipping the Lord.

God has carved out a sanctuary for Himself right in the very core of your being. As soon as you intentionally go into your inner room, you are ushered into the highest place imaginable in the Spirit. It's like an elevator to the top floor that instantly relocates you spiritually into the very throne room of heaven. Your spirit is now fixed in Christ Jesus and as a consequence you are permanently seated in heaven. Your spirit is bi-locational, just like everyday quantum particles.[3] Your spirit can be in two places at one time. It is here on earth inside your physical body and it is in heaven simultaneously.

Because we are in Christ, it is now also just as true of us as it was of Jesus when He described Himself, whilst here on earth, as "The Son of Man who is in heaven" (John 3:13). Because your spirit is permanently located in heaven, you have access to the fullness of the ecstasy and bliss of heaven. The Holy Spirit desires to train us to engage our spirit in such a way that we can access the glory realm of heaven and learn how to allow that atmosphere to spill out of your spirit and overflow into every part of your soul, bringing your mind, will, and emotions under the power and influence of heaven.

The soul of Jesus was comprehensively under the influence of Jesus' spirit at all times. That is why Jesus lived in the fullness of love, joy, peace, and righteousness. The miracle of the new creation opens up extraordinary possibilities of supernatural transformation for those who learn how to engage and activate their spirit and to allow our spirit to rule over every part of our soul. And all of this flows out of the miraculous circumcision of the heart.

Chapter Four

Soul, Spirit, and the Logic of the New Testament

The writer of Hebrews taught that the living and powerful, creative Word of God has literally separated soul from spirit at the new birth. This concept of the separation of soul and spirit is crucial in the development of a clear comprehension of the radicalism of the new creation. The miracle performed upon your human spirit is a finished work, whereas the work God is continuing to do in the regions of your soul is an unfinished work. God is still very much at work within us.

Hebrews 4:12 is a headline verse. Without an understanding of this separation between soul and spirit, our perception of the new creation will always remain a little fuzzy. This separation sheds tremendous light upon the inner dynamics of the new creation and it forms the sub-structure that undergirds all New Testament theology concerning the process of inner transformation. I would like to suggest that the separation of soul and spirit is an implicit understanding that runs through the entire body of New Testament theology and that it was clearly understood by the authors of the New Testament. In that regard, it represents the logic of the New Testament.

In the first chapter of this book, we briefly outlined a vision of the tripartite nature of man. Human beings are made up of three distinct parts: we are a spirit, we have a soul, and we have a body. You and I are spiritual beings because we have a spirit. As a spirit being, you will exist forever. Spirits do not die. James said, "The body without the spirit is dead" (James 2:26). Paul taught that those who die in Christ go straight to be with Christ for eternity. "For to me, to live is Christ and to die is gain. If I am to go on living in the body, this will mean fruitful labour for me. Yet what shall I choose? I do not know! I am torn between the two: I desire to depart and be with Christ, which is better by far; but it is more necessary for you that I remain in the body" (Philippians 1:21-24 NIV). Those who die outside of Christ continue as spirit beings yet separated from God for eternity.

Paul clearly taught that we are tripartite beings. This was fundamental to the entire framework of his new creation theology. "Now may the God of peace make you holy in every way, and may your whole spirit and soul and body be kept blameless until that day when our Lord Jesus Christ comes again" (1 Thessalonians 5:23 NLT). Paul spoke specifically about our human spirit. "But if Christ is in you, your body is dead because of sin, yet your spirit is alive because of righteousness" (Romans 8:10 NIV). It is important to note that it is our spirit that has been made alive to God.

The miracle of the new birth establishes a profound spiritual union between our human spirit and the Spirit of God. "The Spirit himself testifies with our spirit that we are God's children" (Romans 8:16 NIV). "Spirit can be known only by spirit—God's Spirit and our spirits in open communion" (1 Corinthians 2:14 MSG). Paul proclaimed, "He who is joined to the Lord is one spirit with Him" (1 Corinthians 6:17). This is an extraordinary thing: our human spirit, which was once dead to God and alive to sin, has now been supernaturally made gloriously alive to God and dead to sin. This is the actual state of our new human spirit. Your spirit is now alive from the dead!

Paul taught that when Jesus died on the cross, He died to sin. "God made him who had no sin to be sin for us" (2 Corinthians 5:21

NIV). Jesus died for our sins but He also died to sin once and for all. "For the death that He died, He died to sin once for all" (Romans 6:10). When He rose again from the dead, He was made gloriously alive to God. Using the paradigm of the death and resurrection of Christ, Paul then said, "In the same way, count yourselves dead to sin but alive to God in Christ Jesus" (Romans 6:11 NIV). Two chapters later, Paul proclaimed that "your spirit is alive because of righteousness" (Romans 8:10 NIV).

Because you were in Adam, your human spirit was once spiritually dead. In this fallen state your entire being—spirit, soul, and body—became defiled and corrupted by sin. Even our spirit (which before the fall was a sanctuary of the glory of God) became defiled by sin and impurity. But the moment we place our trust in Jesus for salvation, we passed from death to life in our spirit. For those of us who have been demonised, every demon was instantly expelled from our spirit and banished to the, as yet, un-renewed regions of the soul.

Our spirit was suddenly enveloped in the Holy Spirit so that it is now completely "in Christ." Christ Himself becomes like a wall of fire around our human spirit so that our spirit once again becomes the inviolable sanctuary of God. Your spirit is now absolutely sacrosanct! The Lord said concerning the city of Jerusalem, "'For I,' declares the Lord, 'will be a wall of fire around her, and I will be the glory in her midst'" (Zechariah 2:5 NASB). The same could be said of your regenerated human spirit: the Lord is a wall of fire around it and He has immersed your human spirit in His heavenly glory.

Jesus described your spirit as an inner room. The inner room of your spirit is a glorious sanctuary that God invites you to explore. Now that we are new creations, we have the privilege of entering a sanctuary that is filled with the peace, love, joy, and glory of God. God said to the citizens of Jerusalem: "Walk about Zion and go all around her" (Psalm 48:12). In like manner, He invites you to explore the frontiers of your brand new spirit. Your spirit is a vast and expansive region within you. It is not an infinitesimally small quantum particle, a mere dot at the centre of your being. It is the true you, and everything that constitutes the free version of you as a brand new creation of God. "For we are His workmanship; created in Christ Jesus" (Ephesians 2:10). Your new spirit is a masterpiece: an expression of the workmanship of the very Creator of the universe who delights in making all things new.

What a remarkable revelation! This creative work of God at the very core of your being is a miracle. Because your spirit is now alive to God, this means you have been restored to 24/7 open communion with God. Your fellowship with a holy God has been comprehensively restored through one glorious act of God. It is through this miracle that you can go into your inner room anytime you want to commune with your Father in heaven. No matter what depths of depravity you have come from, no matter how broken you are, you can enter into perfect intimate communion with God anytime, anywhere. This explains how a desperately broken person can enjoy the gift of restored fellowship with God from the first day of their salvation.

Your spirit has been supernaturally re-created. Your spirit is sinless and free of evil. Your spirit has been made as righteous before the Father as the spirit of Jesus Himself. God has not just declared you to be righteous in His sight – in fact, your spirit has been made the righteousness of God in Christ Jesus. Your spirit is justified and holy before the Lord. It has an entirely new nature of righteousness and true holiness. Because it is completely holy, it has a nature free from sin. "Whoever has been born of God does not sin for His seed remains in him; and he cannot sin because he has been born of God" (1 John 3:9). Your new nature cannot sin because it is dead to sin and alive to God. It is not a sin nature but a nature governed by righteousness. It is only our foolish, un-renewed choices to align ourselves with sin that entangle us again. Yet even in the midst of sinful and foolish choices, our spirit remains undefiled because it has now been completely immersed in the Spirit of Christ.

There is a debate about whether our renewed spirit is now natural or supernatural in nature. There is no question that the renewing of our spirit is the result of a supernatural agency, but does this mean that we are now supernatural beings by virtue of the new birth? The argument that we are now supernatural beings is built upon two primary Pauline passages. The first support is found in 1 Corinthians 15:48-49, "As was the man of dust, so also are those who are made of dust; and as is the heavenly Man, so also are *those who are heavenly*. And as we have borne the image of the man of dust, we shall also bear the image of the heavenly Man." This passage suggests that we are of an entirely new order of *heavenly* [supernatural] beings by virtue of the new creation.

The second support for this argument is found in Paul's contrast between the natural man and the spiritual man. He said, "The natural man does not receive the things of the Spirit of God, for they are foolishness to him; nor can he know them, because they are spiritually discerned [*anakrino*]. But he who is spiritual judges [*anakrino*] all things; yet he himself is rightly judged [*anakrino*] by no one" (1 Corinthians 1:14-15). The spiritual man is said to be a new supernatural being instead of a natural one. This supernatural man has been fitted with a new capacity to discern [*anakrino*] supernatural realities yet he is of such an entirely new order of spiritual beings that he is not able to be discerned [*anakrino*] by others because of his new heavenly identity. Whether our new spirit is natural or supernatural in nature is open for debate. But one thing is certain: the finished work in our spirit and the unfinished work in our soul forms a theological substructure that undergirds New Testament theology and new creation thinking.

Chapter Five

The Tripartite Tabernacle of Man

The Old Testament Tabernacle is a prophetic picture of the tripartite nature of human beings. The Tabernacle consisted of three distinct parts: the outer court, the holy place, and the holy of holies. These three compartments of the Tabernacle have often been likened to the three compartments of the human being: the body, the soul, and the human spirit. Various New Testament theologians have observed this striking correspondence. One such respected theologian is Ray Stedman who, in his commentary on the book of Hebrews, developed the argument that the pattern of the Tabernacle revealed to Moses in the mountain was, among other things, a pattern of the tripartite nature of man.

Stedman specifically asserts that the reality of the tripartite nature of man "would explain the threefold division of the tabernacle. The 'Outer Court' corresponds to the body, the 'Holy Place' to the soul; and the 'Most Holy Place;' to the spirit."[4] God's intent from the beginning was that man would be the dwelling place of God on the earth, of which, the Tabernacle is but a type and a shadow of these deeper spiritual realities. Whilst the Tabernacle speaks prophetically of other aspects of the relationship between God and humanity, such as our approach to a Holy God, it nevertheless seems to also reflect this tripartite nature of human beings.

Stedman builds his case for the differentiation between spirit, soul, and body by pointing to Paul's statement in 1 Corinthians 6:17, "He who is joined to the Lord is one spirit with Him." Because our human spirit has now been supernaturally welded to the Holy Spirit, our spirit is with Christ in heaven. Stedman points to Ephesians 2:5-6 where Paul says that God has "made us alive together with Christ and raised us up together, and made us sit together in the heavenly places in Christ Jesus." He then goes on to say in his commentary on Hebrews that "this strongly suggests that what Moses saw on the mountain was the human person as we were meant to be; the dwelling place of God – the Holy of Holies."[5]

Stedman also quotes Revelation 21:3, "Behold, the tabernacle [*skene*] of God is with men, and He will dwell with them, and they shall be His people. God Himself will be with them and be their God." According to Paul, "Your body is the temple of the Holy Spirit who is in you" (1 Corinthians 6:19). "For you are the temple of the living God. As God has said, 'I will dwell in them and walk among them. I will be their God and they shall be My people'" (2 Corinthians 6:16).

Stedman writes that Jesus, our Great High Priest, "has found a way to repossess the human spirit and cleanse it with the 'better sacrifice' of Himself and to dwell within forever by means of the Eternal Spirit. This view of the true tabernacle as the human person is also supported by Paul in his description of what awaits believers at death."[6] Paul describes the human body as an earthly tent, which is reminiscent of the language of the Old Testament tabernacle, which was sometimes called a tent. "Now we know that if the earthly tent [skene] we live in is destroyed, we have a building from God, an eternal house in heaven, not built by human hands" (2 Corinthians 5:1 NIV). All of these correspondences between the Old Testament Tabernacle and the tripartite nature of man suggest biblically that the Holy of Holies is the counterpart of the human spirit. Prophetic author, Graham Cooke writes:

God lives in the human spirit. His Holy Spirit mingles with our spirit. Our spirit is only ever subject to, and in the presence of God. It is the part of us which is eternal. It constantly communes with God Himself. It is a place inside of us that cannot be touched by anything out in the world because it lives in the presence of God.[7]

The human spirit is now fully immersed in the Shekinah glory of God. Just as the Holy of Holies in the Old Testament Tabernacle represented the localised presence of the glory of God on earth, so now the regenerated human spirit is the localised presence of God's glory on earth. Human beings were always created to be the dwelling place of God. The fall of man saw God expelled from the human spirit and the spirit was rendered dead to God. Ray Stedman explains:

The true sanctuary [Holy of Holies] is the realm of the spirit in man. It is pictured in the Tabernacle. We have the outer court in the body, the holy place in the soul, and the holy of holies is the spirit of man. It was this into which we were forbidden to enter as long as we did not know Jesus Christ. We could not move into the realm of the spirit. Our spirits, the Bible says, "were dead in trespasses and sins" (Ephesians 2:1). But through the blood of Christ a way has been opened into this area. When we became Christians, for the first time we were able to operate on a spiritual level. Our spirits began to function. We became, for the first time, complete human beings, operating as God intended man to operate. It is this inner man that the writer is referring to as the sanctuary. We now come with boldness, he says, into the inner man, into the realm of the spirit, where we meet face to face with God. The spirit is the only part of man that can meet God.[8]

Because we are alive to God, our spirit is now in a state of permanent union and communion with Him. "Spirit can be known only by spirit—God's Spirit and our spirits in open communion"

(1 Corinthians 2:14 MSG). This state is unchanging because our spirit is now completely free of sin and is permanently joined to the Holy Spirit. In a previous chapter we saw that Jesus said, "But you, when you pray, go into your inner room, close your door, and pray to your Father who is in secret, and your Father who sees what is done in secret will reward you openly" (Matthew 6:6 NASB). This inner room is the new Holy of Holies: the inner man or woman of the spirit. The human spirit is now completely holy in Christ. It is perfect in every way: it is righteous, it is pure, it is blameless, and it is comprehensively sanctified and cleansed. It must be perfect so that it can be joined to the Lord and immersed into the Holy Spirit.

However, as Watchman Nee points out in his book, *Release of the Spirit*, the soul life must be comprehensively renewed and made holy through the power of the cross so that the human spirit may be released and expressed through every part of us. This revelation explains the paradox between who we are in Christ and who we are becoming. According to Watchman Nee:

> When God comes to indwell us, by His Spirit, life and pow-
> er, He comes into our spirit which we are calling the inward
> man. Outside of this inward man is the soul wherein func-
> tions our thoughts, emotions and will. The outermost man is
> our physical body. Thus we will speak of the inward man as
> the spirit, the outer man as the soul and the outermost man
> as the body. We must know that he who can work for God
> is the one whose inward man is released. Our spirit seems to
> be wrapped in a covering so that it cannot easily break forth.
> The Lord wants to break our outward man in order that the
> inward man may have a way out. When the inward man is
> released, both unbelievers and Christians will be blessed.[9]

This tripartite picture of the three compartments of the human being is particularly helpful in understanding how we can enter into intimate communion with Father, Son, and Holy Spirit from the very moment of conversion and regeneration. There is a perfect sanctuary within each born again believer that is thoroughly cleansed and perfected by the blood of Jesus. We may enter into that sanctuary, by faith, to commune with God, enjoy all the blessings of our new life in Christ, and taste the fullness of the Holy Spirit. But meanwhile, in the Holy Place and the Outer Court, the soul and the body are still being systematically brought into subjection to "the Father of spirits" (Hebrews 12:9). We will explore this theme further in a later chapter.

Interestingly, the Holy Place (which represents the soul) was furnished with the table of showbread, the altar of incense, and the golden lampstand. The table of showbread spoke of Christ, the bread of life (John 6:35). The incense spoke of Christ as the aroma of life (2 Corinthians 2:15,16), and the golden lampstand spoke of Christ as the light of life (John 8:12). This light, this fragrance of hot baked bread, and this sweet smelling incense permeated every part of the Holy Place, indicating that God intends His life to permeate every part of our soul so that it becomes holy unto the Lord. As the light of the glory and the fragrance of heaven permeates our souls, every part of our mind, will, and emotions become holy, just as our spirit was made holy at the moment of our regeneration.

Notice also the strong sensory element of the physical features within the Holy Place. The golden lampstand fills the room with a dancing light from the seven flames that represent the seven-fold Spirit of God. The flickering light reflected off the walls of the Holy Place because these walls were covered with gold. This impacts our sense of sight. Next, there was the fragrance of burning incense crackling upon the coals that are perpetually maintained by the High Priest on the golden altar. The sound and smell of smouldering coals, and the fragrance of sweet smelling incense, assault the senses of smell and hearing. Similarly, the showbread releases that all too familiar bakery smell, which tantalises the taste buds. All of these physical realities— the three pieces of golden furniture glistening in the light from the lampstand, the fresh bread, the oil in the seven lamps, the fragrant incense, the smoking coals, and the flickering light—all impact the sensory realm, which represents the interface between the soul and the physical world.

There is an important distinction to be made between the Holy of Holies and the Holy Place. The Holy of Holies was absolutely holy whereas the Holy Place was only *relatively* holy. The Holy of Holies was inhabited exclusively by God alone every day of the year except for the Day of Atonement. On this most holy day of the Jewish calendar, only the High Priest could enter the Holy of Holies. The High Priest could only enter after an elaborate ceremony through which he made atonement for the sins of the children of Israel by sprinkling fresh blood upon the mercy seat. This prophetically prefigured the atonement of Christ, our Great High Priest, who entered the true heavenly Holy of Holies on the ultimate Day of Atonement as our Forerunner.

By way of contrast, the Holy Place was visited regularly by the High Priest and the Levites engaged in servicing the tabernacle. They would enter this room daily to replenish the lampstand with oil, keep the incense burning upon the altar, and replace the showbread. In this sense, the Holy Place was regularly defiled by sin as the priests were certainly not sinless and perfect. Subsequently, the Holy Place represented the intersection of heaven and earth. It was one step closer to the absolute holiness manifested in the Holy of Holies, but it was nevertheless defiled by the presence of fallen man. This is an important truth for us as we contemplate the distinction between the regenerated human spirit and the soul of the believer. The soul is a mixture of the sanctifying influences of the Spirit and the unholy defilement of residual sin.

Our renewed spirit is completely undefiled and holy. There is nothing more that God can do for the human spirit because it has been perfected by God and made righteous before Him. It cannot be contaminated by sin since it is in Christ and has been purified and comprehensively cleansed. Not so the soul. It is being cleansed and sanctified but it is still defiled by sin. The influence of the light, the life, and the love of Christ is present in the Holy Place of the soul, but there is still need for the Christian to repent and to confess their sin because of the ongoing influence of the presence of sin in the soul.

The Apostle John said, "If we say that we have no sin, we deceive ourselves, and the truth is not in us. If we say that we have not sinned, we make Him a liar, and His word is not in us" (1 John 1:8-10). This is why James said, "Confess your sins to each other and pray for each other so that you may be healed" (James 5:16 NLT). Jesus taught His followers to regularly pray, "Forgive us our sins, just as we have forgiven those who have sinned against us" (Matthew 6:12 NLT). We are all given the assurance that "If we confess our sins, He is faithful and just to forgive us our sins and to cleanse us from all unrighteousness" (1 John 1:9).

For many years, I had been perplexed by the paradox of why a Christian still has to confess their sins even though Jesus has "washed us from our sins in His own blood" (Revelation 1:5). On the one hand, Christians have "washed their robes and made them white in the blood of the Lamb" (Revelation 7:14), yet there is a continuing imperative to confess and forsake our sins. We sing songs that celebrate the fact that our sins have all been washed away, yet we must still confess our sins to God and ask for forgiveness from God. We will address this paradox in greater detail in chapter ten, but it is important to mention it at this point because the Old Testament tabernacle has many powerful prophetic insights for us to draw upon. The answer, of course, lies in the separation of soul and spirit. The Holy place is still defiled by sin whilst the Holy of Holies remains in that state of being permanently washed and cleansed.

We must allow the light of life, the aroma of life and the bread of life to continually permeate every room within the soul until our entire mind, will, and emotions are purged of sin and death. God wants the life of Christ to permeate and renew every part of our mind. "If your sinful nature controls your mind, there is death. But if the Holy Spirit controls your mind, there is life and peace" (Romans 8:6 NLT). In like manner, when rebellion and disobedience controls our will there is death, but when the Spirit controls our will there is life and peace. The same could be said of our emotions. Negative and destructive emotions produce spiritual death in our soul. Because of the new birth, our spirit is alive to God. Now God wants that same life to permeate and infiltrate every area of the soul that has been under the reign of death.

The light of the glory of God that illuminates our understanding, the sweet-smelling fragrance of Christ that replaces the aroma of death, and the bread of heaven that nourishes and gives life to the soul, are all Christological realities from "within the veil." Yet these things must permeate the outer life of the soul until every part of our soul life is brought under the rule and reign of this great salvation. "We are not of those who draw back to perdition, but of those who believe to the saving of the soul" (Hebrews 10:39). "Though you have not seen Him, you love Him, and though you do not see Him now, but believe in Him, you greatly rejoice with joy inexpressible and full of glory, obtaining as the outcome of your faith: the salvation of your souls" (1 Peter 1:8-9 NASB). The Greek word for salvation comes from the root word *sozo*, which can be translated, "healing or being made whole." This verse could legitimately be rendered as "the healing of your soul."

It is through faith and obedience to the word of God that we enter into the experiential reality of this glorious salvation in every part of our mind, will, and emotions. The language used by the writers of the New Testament would suggest that they were all established in the revelation that the spirit is already saved but the soul is being saved; the spirit is already sanctified but the soul is being sanctified, and that the spirit is already perfect but the soul is being perfected.

The challenge for the believer is to walk by faith in the light of the revelation of who we now are in Christ, persevering until we see these realties established in every area of our souls. The mind, will, and emotions of Jesus were under the complete governance of His spirit, and this is the pattern we are to pursue in our own interior life. Biblically, we are called to live from the reality that in our spirit we are new creations: old things have passed away and all things have become new. We are called to align ourselves with the revelation of our new identity in Christ, as men and women who are now made alive to God and dead to sin and live from that prophetic perspective. Meanwhile, in the "outer world" of the soul, our mind, will, and emotions are being transformed and brought progressively into a greater conformity with who we are in our inner spirit.

We are called to live from our spirit man rather than from our soul. To do this, we must learn to engage with our spirit man who lives deep within the Holy of Holies with Jesus. This is the true "you" because you are an eternal spirit being who has been gloriously regenerated. Nevertheless, the writer of Hebrews calls us to experientially enter the Holy of Holies. He speaks of those "who have fled for refuge to lay hold of the hope set before us. This hope we have as an anchor of the soul, both sure and steadfast, and which enters the Presence behind the veil, where the Forerunner has entered for us, even Jesus" (Hebrews 6:18-20). Jesus entered the Most Holy Place as our Great High Priest, and now we are called to follow Him so that we experientially enter into a life *within the veil*.

Jesus continually prays that we will experientially enter the Holy of Holies: "Father, I desire that they also whom You gave Me may be with Me where I am, that they may behold My glory" (John 17:24). Where is Jesus? According to the previous quote from Hebrews, He is in the Most Holy Place. That is where He is calling us through His endless intercession.

"Therefore, brothers, since we have confidence to enter the Most Holy Place by the blood of Jesus, by a new and living way opened for us through the curtain, that is, His body, and since we have a Great Priest over the house of God, let us draw near to God with a sincere heart in full assurance of faith" (Hebrews 10:19-22 NIV).

Those who enter by faith within the veil learn to live from the perspective that our spirit is joined to the Lord within the Holy of Holies and that we are now one with Him. Everything else becomes peripheral to this singular reality. Even though the storms that rage in the un-renewed areas of the soul have become peripheral to the man or woman in Christ, we must avoid the error of living in denial of those un-renewed aspects of the soul. They are still realities that must be addressed if our souls are to be conformed to the image of Christ. God is not in denial about the strongholds of the mind, the will, and the emotions. He is focused upon cleansing, healing, and purifying the soul so that the glory of the inner man shines through every area of our soul. That is why God searches the heart and mind!

Chapter Six

The Paradox of Sanctification

In New Testament theology we are confronted by a set of interesting paradoxes. A paradox consists of two seemingly contradictory statements that are both nevertheless true. There is a profound paradox that weaves a thread throughout all of Paul's, John's, and Peter's theology concerning who we are in Christ and who it is that we are becoming, and between what God has already done as a finished work in our hearts and what He is still doing. I have compiled a list of some of these great theological paradoxes so you can see what I mean. I encourage you to read them thoughtfully so that you can see for yourself these startling theological paradoxes. I assure you, the fruit of this exercise will be considerably rewarding because it brings into focus a powerful biblical truth that enables us to see even deeper into the nature of the new creation miracle.

1. We are saved.

- By this gospel you are saved (1 Corinthians 15:2 NIV).

- For it is with your heart that you believe and are justified, and it is with your mouth that you confess and are saved (Romans 10:10).

We are being saved.

- For the message of the cross is foolishness to those who are perishing, but to us who are being saved it is the power of God (1 Corinthians 1:18).

- For we are to God the fragrance of Christ among those who are being saved and among those who are perishing (2 Corinthians 2:15).

2. We are sanctified in Christ.

- To the church of God which is at Corinth, to those who are sanctified in Christ Jesus (1 Corinthians 1:2).

- But you were washed, but you were sanctified, but you were justified in the name of the Lord Jesus and by the Spirit of our God (1 Corinthians 6:11).

We are being sanctified.

- For both He who sanctifies and those who are being sanctified are all of one, for which reason He is not ashamed to call them brethren (Hebrews 2:11).

- For by one offering He has perfected forever those who are being sanctified (Hebrews 10:14).

3. We are saints.

- Paul, an apostle of Jesus Christ by the will of God, to the saints who are in Ephesus, and faithful in Christ Jesus (Ephesians 1:1).

We are called to be saints.

- To all who are in Rome, beloved of God, called to be saints (Romans 1:7).

4. We are complete in Christ.

- You are complete in Him, who is the head of all principality and power (Colossians 2:10).

We are being brought to completion.

- Being confident of this, that he who began a good work in you will carry it on to completion until the day of Christ Jesus (Philippians 1:6 NIV).

- Let patience have its perfect work, that you may be perfect and complete, lacking nothing (James 1:4).

- Finally, brethren, farewell. Become complete (2 Corinthians 13:11).

- But may the God of all grace, who called us to His eternal glory by Christ Jesus ... perfect, establish, strengthen, and settle you (1 Peter 5:10).

The Greek word for perfect is *katartizo*, which means "to be brought to completion or thoroughly completed."

5. We are perfect in Christ.

- For by one offering He has perfected forever those who are being sanctified (Hebrews 10:14).

- But you have come to Mount Zion and to the city of the living God, the heavenly Jerusalem, to an innumerable company of angels, to the general assembly and church of the firstborn who are registered in heaven, to God the Judge of all, to the spirits of just men made perfect (Hebrews 12:22-23).

- I sleep, but my heart is awake; It is the voice of my beloved! He knocks, saying, "Open for me, my sister, my love, My dove, my perfect one; for my head is covered with dew, My locks with the drops of the night" (Song of Songs 5:2).

We are being perfected.

- Him we preach, warning every man and teaching every man in all wisdom, that we may present every man perfect in Christ Jesus (Colossians 1:28).

- Therefore, leaving the discussion of the elementary principles of Christ, let us go on to perfection (Hebrews 6:1).

- Therefore, having these promises, beloved, let us cleanse ourselves from all filthiness of the flesh and spirit, perfecting holiness in the fear of God (2 Corinthians 7:1).

- Not that I have already attained, or am already perfected; but I press on, that I may lay hold of that for which Christ Jesus has also laid hold of me (Philippians 3:12).

- There is no fear in love; but perfect love casts out fear, because fear involves torment. But he who fears has not been made perfect in love (1 John 4:18).

- Having begun by the Spirit, are you now being perfected by the flesh (Galatians 3:3 NASB)?

- I in them, and You in Me; that they may be made perfect in one (John 17:23).

6. We are holy in Christ.

- But now he has reconciled you by Christ's physical body through death to present you holy in his sight, without blemish and free from accusation (Colossians 1:22 NIV).

- Therefore, holy brethren, partakers of the heavenly calling.... (Hebrews 3:1).

We are called to be holy.

- To the church of God in Corinth, to those sanctified in Christ Jesus and called to be holy (1 Corinthians 1:2 NIV).

- He has saved us and called us to a holy life (2 Timothy 1:9 NIV).

- And may the Lord make you increase and abound in love to one another and to all, just as we do to you, so that He may establish your hearts blameless in holiness before our God and Father at the coming of our Lord Jesus Christ with all His saints (1 Thessalonians 3:13).

- Let us cleanse ourselves from all filthiness of the flesh and spirit, perfecting holiness in the fear of God (2 Corinthians 7:1).

7. We are blameless before God.

- Just as He chose us in Him before the foundation of the world, that we should be holy and without blame before Him in love (Ephesians 1:4).

We are called to be blameless.

- Do everything without complaining or arguing, so that you may become blameless and pure (Philippians 2:14-15).

- So then, dear friends, since you are looking forward to this, make every effort to be found spotless, blameless and at peace with him (2 Peter 3:14).

8. We are the righteousness of God in Christ.

- God made him who had no sin to be sin for us, so that in him we might become the righteousness of God (2 Corinthians 5:21).

We are called to pursue righteousness.

- Flee also youthful lusts; but pursue righteousness, faith, love, peace (2 Timothy 2:22).

9. We are already new in Christ.

- Therefore, if anyone is in Christ, he is a new creation; old things have passed away; behold, all things have become new (2 Corinthians 5:17).

We are being renewed day by day.

- You have clothed yourselves with a brand-new nature that is continually being renewed as you learn more and more about Christ, who created this new nature within you (Colossians 3:10 NLT).

- Even though our outward man is perishing, yet the inward man is being renewed day by day (2 Corinthians 4:16).

- Be renewed in the spirit of your mind (Ephesians 4:23).

- Do not be conformed to this world, but be transformed by the renewing of your mind (Romans 12:2).

10. We are clean in Christ.

- You are already clean because of the word which I have spoken to you (John 15:3).

We are being cleansed.

- Christ loved the church and gave himself up for her to make her holy, cleansing her by the washing with water through the word, and to present her to himself as a radiant church, without stain or wrinkle or any other blemish, but holy and blameless (Ephesians 5:25-27).

- Therefore, having these promises, beloved, let us cleanse ourselves from all filthiness of the flesh and spirit, perfecting holiness in the fear of God (2 Corinthians 7:1).

11. We are pure in Christ.

- God alone made it possible for you to be in Christ Jesus. For our benefit God made Christ to be wisdom itself. He is the one who made us acceptable to God. He made us pure and holy (1 Corinthians 1:30 NLT).

- To the pure [katharos] all things are pure, but to those who are defiled and unbelieving nothing is pure (Titus 1:15).

We are being purified.

- Everyone who has this hope in Him purifies himself, just as He is pure (1 John 3:3).

- Since you have purified your souls in obeying the truth through the Spirit in sincere love of the brethren, love one another fervently with a pure heart (1 Peter 1:22).

- Purify your hearts, you double-minded (James 4:8).

12. We are faultless in Christ.

- These are the ones who were not defiled with women, for they are virgins. These are the ones who follow the Lamb wherever He goes. These were redeemed from among men, being first-fruits to God and to the Lamb. And in their mouth was found no deceit, for they are without fault before the throne of God (Revelation 14:4-5).

We are called to be faultless.

- Do all things without complaining and disputing, that you may become blameless and harmless, children of God without fault in the midst of a crooked and perverse generation, among whom you shine as lights in the world (Philippians 2:14-15).

13. We have already received fullness in Christ.

- And of His fullness we have all received, and grace for grace (John 1:16).

- For in Christ all the fullness of the Deity lives in bodily form, and you have been given fullness in Christ (Colossians 2:10 NIV).

We are being filled with His fullness.

- Till we all come to the unity of the faith and of the knowledge of the Son of God, to a perfect man, to the measure of the stature of the fullness of Christ (Ephesians 4:19).

- To know the love of Christ which passes knowledge; that you may be filled with all the fullness of God (Ephesians 3:19).

14. Christ is in you through the new birth.

- Do you not know yourselves; that Jesus Christ is in you (2 Corinthians 13:5)?

Christ is still being formed in you.

- My little children, for whom I labour in birth again until Christ is formed in you (Galatians 4:19).

- For whom He foreknew, He also predestined to be conformed [summorphos] to the image of His Son, that He might be the firstborn among many brethren (Romans 8:29).

- Do not be conformed to this world, but be transformed [metamorphoo] by the renewing of your mind (Romans 12:2).

- But we all, with unveiled face, beholding as in a mirror the glory of the Lord, are being transformed [metamorphoo] into the same image from glory to glory, just as by the Spirit of the Lord (2 Corinthians 3:18).

We understand from these verses that there is a finished work of the Spirit in our human spirit, and there is also an unfinished work of the Spirit in the ongoing, progressive transformation of our souls. There can be no doubt that Paul understood this and that this deliberate separation of soul and spirit forms the sub-structure and the logic of Paul's theology of personal transformation. Once we accept that this is the logic of Paul's theology and indeed of all the Apostles, the New Testament makes even more sense when we encounter these theological paradoxes. From these 14 points we can derive the following chart:

Finished Work in our Human Spirit	Unfinished Work in our Soul
1. We are saved.	We are being saved
2. We are santified	We are being sanctified
3. We are saints	We are called to be saints
4. We are complete in Christ	We are being completed
5. We are perfect in Christ	We are being perfected
6. We are holy in Christ	We are called to be holy
7. We are blameless in Christ	We are becoming blameless
8. We are righteous in Christ	We are called to be righteous
9. We are new in Christ	We are being renewed
10. We are clean in Christ	We are being cleansed
11. We are pure in Christ	We are being purified
12. We are faultless in Christ	We are called to be faultless
13. We have received fullness	We are called to be filled
14. We are indwelt by Christ	Christ is being formed in us

How Do We Explain These Paradoxes?

These paradoxes exist in the New Testament, and especially in Pauline Theology, because every follower of Christ is called to live a life that is consistent with who they have now become in Christ as a result of the new birth. Our souls (our mind, will, and emotions) are being brought into alignment with our renewed spirit. The life that has already been imparted to our human spirit must permeate every un-renewed area of the soul until everything is made new. Paul deliberately differentiated between the spirit, soul, and body, and he prayed that each part of us would be completely sanctified.

"May God himself, the God of peace, sanctify you through and through. May your whole spirit, soul and body be kept blameless at the coming of our Lord Jesus Christ. The one who calls you is faithful and He will do it" (1 Thessalonians 5:23-24 NIV). It would be rather disingenuous of Paul to pray for something which had already taken place. Paul focuses upon the faithfulness of God in His promise to do what He said He would do. "Being confident of this, that he who began a good work in you will carry it on to completion until the day of Christ Jesus" (Philippians 1:6 NIV).

The work of sanctification continues in the region of the human soul [mind, will and emotions] but the spirit of all regenerated sons and daughters of God has already been perfected and sanctified. Peter commended the audience of his first epistle because they had purified their souls of all hatred and bitterness and had attained a place of pure love for their brethren. "Since you have in obedience to the truth purified [*hagnizo*] your souls for a sincere love of the brethren, fervently love one another from a pure heart" (1 Peter 1:22 NASB). The transition from a life of rebellion to a life of obedience to the truth is the key to the sanctification of the soul. It is only as we take back ground forfeited to the enemy of our souls through our minds being progressively renewed by the truth that we can re-occupy all the places that have been captured by the powers of darkness.

Peter used the Greek word *hagnizo* to denote the purification process of the soul. Hagnizo is a verb form of *hagios* [holy], and it means to make clean or to sanctify. Hagnizo is closely related to hag*iazo*. Therefore it would be appropriate to speak of the sanctification of the soul that takes place through our obedience to the truth and the washing of the water of the word. John uses the same word 'hagnizo' in his first epistle. "Everyone who has this hope in Him purifies [hagnizo] himself, just as He is pure" (1 John 3:3). Similarly, James says, "Purify [hagnizo] your hearts, you double-minded" (James 4:8).

New Testament writers often echoed the language of the "water of Purification," which purified both the sanctuary and those who entered it. Paul tells us that "Christ also loved the church and gave Himself for her, that He might sanctify and cleanse her with the **washing of water** by the word, that He might present her to Himself a glorious church, not having spot or wrinkle or any such thing, but that she should be holy and without blemish" (Ephesians 5:25-27). There is a necessity for all believers to cleanse themselves in order for their souls to be purified of sin. "In a large house there are articles not only of gold and silver, but also of wood and clay; some are for noble purposes and some for ignoble. If a man **cleanses himself** from the latter, he will be an instrument for noble purposes, made holy, useful to the Master" (2 Timothy 2:20-21 NIV). "Therefore, having these promises, beloved, **let us cleanse ourselves** from all filthiness of the flesh and spirit, perfecting holiness in the fear of God" (2 Corinthians 7:1).

For the believer who is growing spiritually, the soul is now a region that is a strange mixture of both renewed and un-renewed thoughts, healthy and unhealthy emotions, and pockets of rebellion and submission in the arena of the will. It is a mixture because it is still being sanctified and cleansed through the systematic transformation of the mind, will, and emotions. The interior life of Jesus the man is the pattern of wholeness for each of us who are being conformed to His image. Thank God we have a template! Because Jesus was absolutely perfect in His spirit, soul, and body, the full glory of the Father residing in His spirit could shine and refract through the uniqueness of His personality. Our spirit has been supernaturally perfected and made righteous before the Father. Just like the spirit of Jesus, God has imparted His own nature of righteousness to our spirit. But our soul, unlike the perfect soul of Jesus, still needs to be washed, cleansed, purified, sanctified, and perfected.

For us, these regions of the mind, will, and emotions are being systematically brought into subjection to the rule and reign of the Holy Spirit as the power of God's holiness extends and permeates out from the human spirit to every area of the soul life. Every area of the soul must be freed from the dictates of the old selfish life of the flesh and brought into conformity to the very image of the soul of Christ. Our souls are being restored by the renewing influences of the Holy Spirit. When Paul says, "Inwardly we are being renewed day by day" (2 Corinthians 4:16), he is referring to this process through which every area of our soul is systematically being made new. As David said, "He restores my soul" (Psalm 23:3).

The Greek word Paul used for renewed is *anakainoo*, and it speaks of the application of this newness of life to every area of the soul. It speaks of the removal of everything that constitutes the old nature from the mind, will, and emotions. Paul tells everyone who is a new creation in Christ to "put on the new self, which is being renewed [anakainoo] in knowledge in the image of its Creator" (Colossians 3:10). He tells us to "be transformed by the renewing [anakainosis] of your mind" (Romans 12:2). This *anakainosis* is a process whereby the old is experientially demolished and the reality of the new creation is established in every part of our mind, will, and emotions.

Paul pioneered the concept of believers being *established* in all that God has already wrought in the human spirit. "May the Lord make you increase and abound in love to one another and to all, just as we do to you, so that He may **establish your hearts blameless in holiness** before our God and Father" (1 Thessalonians 3:13). Every born again believer needs to be fully established in holiness, just as their spirit is holy. Paul used the Greek word *sterizo* [establish] to describe this process. *Sterizo* means to be consolidated or to be made solid or stable. *Sterizo* describes the work of God in the soul subsequent to regeneration. "The Lord is faithful, who will **establish** you and guard you from the evil one" (2 Thessalonians 3:3). Paul said, "I am sure that God, who began the good work within you, will continue his work until it is finally finished on that day when Christ Jesus comes back again" (Philippians 1:6).

James indicated that there is still a residue of wickedness in the soul of the believer that needs to be cleansed. I love the quaint turn of phrase used in the Old King James Bible: "Wherefore lay apart all filthiness and *superfluity of naughtiness*, and receive with meekness the engrafted word, which is able to save your souls" (James 1:21 KJV). Other translations read as such: "Therefore lay aside all filthiness and overflow of wickedness" (NKJV), "Putting aside all filthiness and all that remains of wickedness" (NASB), "So get rid of all the filth and evil in your lives" (NLT). This is what Peter calls the "fleshly lusts which war against the soul" (1 Peter 2:11). James called it "your desires for pleasure that war in your members" (James 4:1). Paul said, "For the flesh lusts against the Spirit, and the Spirit against the flesh; and these are contrary to one another" (Galatians 5:17). James said to believers: "purify [*hagnizo*] your hearts, you double-minded" (James 4:8). The writers of the New Testament make it clear that there is still a residue of evil in the soul of the believer that needs to be cleansed and washed away by the power of the blood of Christ.

The paradox of sanctification is that our spirit has been comprehensively purged of sin and rendered evil-free, whereas our soul is being progressively purged of all evil influences. Our spirit is entirely sanctified, but our soul is *being* sanctified. This is the language of the inspired authors of the New Testament. The separation of soul and spirit, wrought by the creative Word of God at new birth, is a powerful New Testament revelation that undergirds and explains the miracle that God has manifested in our spirit. This is a foundational stream of revelation that assists us to understand what has already taken place in our hearts and what remains to be done in our hearts through the sanctifying power of God's Word.

In the following five chapters we will explore what God has done exclusively within the spirit of born again believers. God has:

• Regenerated our human spirit and made it alive to God.

• Imparted the free gift of His own righteousness.

• Made us partakers of His own divine nature.

• Immersed our human spirit within the Spirit of Christ, and

• Given us an entirely new core identity.

There may be some repetition in these chapters because, as I explained in the introduction, we will be examining the work of the new creation from a number of different camera angles. This inevitably leads to a degree of repetition, because we are examining the same miracle from multiple perspectives. But it is only as we interlock these revelations that the full glory of the new creation miracle comes into clear focus. So please bear with this overlap and allow it to reinforce these powerful new creation realities.

Chapter Seven

The "Washing" of Regeneration

I will sprinkle clean water on you, and you shall be clean;
I will cleanse you from all your filthiness. I will give you a
new heart and put a new spirit within you.

(Ezekiel 36:25-26)

God's amazing solution to the problem of sin and the deep separation it brings between man and a holy God is to regenerate the human spirit of all those who simply put their trust in Him. The key passage where Paul develops his theology of supernatural spiritual regeneration is in the epistle to Titus.

> But when the kindness and love of God our Saviour appeared, He saved us, not by works of righteousness which we have done, but according to His mercy He saved us, through the washing of regeneration and renewing of the Holy Spirit, whom He poured out on us abundantly through Jesus Christ our Saviour, that having been justified by His grace we should become heirs according to the hope of eternal life. (Titus 3:4-7)

There is a part of us that is now entirely washed, sanctified, justified, and made alive to God and dead to sin. The miracle of regeneration occurs exclusively in our human spirit. As we saw in chapter two, the Old Testament promised that a day would come when God would put a *new spirit* within us.

> For I will take you from among the nations, gather you out of all countries, and bring you into your own land. Then I will sprinkle clean water on you, and you shall be clean; I will cleanse you from all your filthiness and from all your idols. I will give you a new heart and put a new spirit within you; I will take the heart of stone out of your flesh and give you a heart of flesh. I will put My Spirit within you and cause you to walk in My statutes, and you will keep My judgments and do them. Then you shall dwell in the land that I gave to your fathers; you shall be My people, and I will be your God. (Ezekiel 36:24-28)

Paul deliberately used the phrase "washing of regeneration and renewing" because God had promised to wash us and cleanse us from all our filthiness. This washing of our human spirit is what makes it brand new. This supernatural washing is a one-time event never to be repeated. It is a finished work. Paul described this washing as a past tense operation of the Spirit of God.

> Do you not know that the unrighteous will not inherit the kingdom of God? Do not be deceived. Neither fornicators, nor idolaters, nor adulterers, nor homosexuals, nor sodomites, nor thieves, nor covetous, nor drunkards, nor revilers, nor extortioners will inherit the kingdom of God. And such were some of you. ***But you were washed***, but you were sanctified, but you were justified in the name of the Lord Jesus and by the Spirit of our God. (1 Corinthians 6:9-11)

John said, "To Him who loved us and washed us from our sins in His own blood and has made us kings and priests to His God and Father; to Him be glory and dominion forever and ever" (Revelation 1:5-6). This spiritual washing is a comprehensive washing from all sin so that our spirit is no longer defiled by sin. "Christ loved the church and gave Himself up for her, so that He might sanctify her, *having cleansed her by the washing of water* with the Word; that He might present to Himself the church in all her glory, having no spot or wrinkle or any such thing; but that she would be holy and blameless" (Ephesians 5:25-27 NASB).

We are washed through the prophetic declaration of God as He speaks over our spirit the moment we believe. Jesus said to the disciples, "You are already clean because of the word which I have spoken to you" (John 15:3). You will remember the story of Jesus cleansing the leper. He simply said, "'Be clean!' and immediately his leprosy was cleansed" (Matthew 8:3). In like manner, God speaks His word over the new believer and he is comprehensively cleansed by the power of that creative word. God prophetically declares, "Be made new!" and our spirit is supernaturally renewed! Peter says we "have been born again, not of corruptible seed but incorruptible, through the word of God which lives and abides forever" (1 Peter 1:23). The washing of regeneration cleanses our spirit from all sin. Our spirit is comprehensively washed through the word that God speaks over us. This is a never to be repeated event, and it is a finished work in the very core of our heart!

Our spirit is now brand spanking new! When Paul says, "Therefore, if anyone is in Christ, he is a new creation; old things have passed away; behold, all things have become new" (2 Corinthians 5:17), he is referring to the finished work, which the Holy Spirit has wrought in our human spirit. What does it mean to have a new spirit? Everything that constituted the old has now passed away. Your spirit was dead to God because of the defilement of sin. "As for you, you were dead in your transgressions and sins" (Ephesians 2:1 NIV). "Once you were dead, doomed forever because of your many sins" (NLT).

God gave Ezekiel a powerful vision of this resurrection life that gave rise to the army of New Testament born again believers in the vision of the valley of dry bones.

> Then he said to me, "Prophesy to the breath; prophesy, son of man, and say to it, 'This is what the Sovereign Lord says: "Come from the four winds, O breath, and breathe into these slain, that they may live [*chayah*]."' So I prophesied as He commanded me, and breath entered them; they came to life [*chayah*] and stood up on their feet – an exceedingly great army! (Ezekiel 37:9-10 NIV)[10]

The New Covenant was to be known prophetically as the era of the resurrected ones who have passed from death to life. God said that this resurrection from the dead would occur as God put His Spirit within the hearts of those who believe. The next verse in Ezekiel says:

> Then He said to me, "Son of man, these bones are the whole house of Israel. They indeed say, 'Our bones are dry, our hope is lost, and we ourselves are cut off!' Therefore prophesy and say to them, 'Thus says the Lord God: "Behold, O My people, I will open your graves and cause you to come up from your graves.... Then you shall know that I am the Lord, when I have opened your graves, O My people, and brought you up from your graves. I will put My Spirit in you, and you shall live [chayah]. Then you shall know that I, the Lord, have spoken it and performed it," says the Lord. (Ezekiel 37:11-14)

The Hebrew word for life is *chay*. *Chayah* is an adjective that means "the act of bringing something back to life which was dead." That is exactly what God said He would do to the spirits of the humble and repentant: He would revive or bring them back from the dead. Resurrection is the defining feature of the New Covenant era. This is the foundation of spiritual revival. In fact, all true spiritual renewal springs forth from the revelation that God has already revived us from the dead. A revived church is one that is living experientially in a state of authentic renewal, awake to the revelation that there is already a "big tent revival" going on inside of every believer by virtue of the indwelling of the Holy Spirit. Through the miracle of regeneration, you are now gloriously alive to God.

Paul said, "But because of His great love for us, God, who is rich in mercy, *made us alive* with Christ even when we were dead in our sins – it is by grace you have been saved" (Ephesians 2:4-5). As we have already seen, your spirit is now one hundred percent alive to God. This is now a permanent state of new life in Christ. We have been raised from the dead spiritually. Your spirit is also now one hundred percent dead to sin. Sin has been purged and driven out of your spirit. Paul powerfully expounds on the brand new condition of our spirit in Christ in Romans 6:

> How shall we who died to sin live any longer in it? Or do you not know that as many of us as were baptized into Christ Jesus were baptized into His death? Therefore we were buried with Him through baptism into death, that just as Christ was raised from the dead by the glory of the Father, even so we also should walk in newness of life. For if we have been united together in the likeness of His death, certainly we also shall be in the likeness of His resurrection, knowing this, that our old man was crucified with Him, that the body of sin might be done away with, that we should no longer be slaves of sin. For he who has died has been freed from sin. Now if we died with Christ, we believe that we shall also live with Him, knowing that Christ, having been raised from the dead, dies no more. Death no longer has dominion over Him. For the death that He died, He died to sin once for all; but the life that He lives, He lives to God. Likewise you also, reckon yourselves to be dead indeed to sin, but alive to God in Christ Jesus our Lord. (Romans 6:1-11)

Paul says to those who have a new spirit: "Consider yourselves to be dead to sin and alive to God in Christ Jesus (NASB). Regard it to be absolutely true; it is an accurate description of who you are in your spirit. This is the foundation from which we live our lives as Christians. There is no other foundation upon which we can live. As born again believers, we share in the resurrection life of Jesus Christ. The victory has already been gloriously won through the cross and the new birth. The beachhead has already been established, and the rest of our life is nothing more than a "mopping up operation." This is not to make light of the ongoing process of what Peter calls the "purifying of our souls" (1Peter1:22), but we cannot overstate the greatness of what God has wrought in our human spirits.

The allied forces began flooding onto Omaha beach at Normandy on the shores of France on June 6, 1944. After the loss of many lives, they ultimately established a beachhead in Nazi occupied France. On the first day of the D-Day invasion, nine thousand marines lost their lives but one hundred thousand soldiers managed to land. Once the beachhead was established, they were able to move in the heavy equipment and the hundreds of thousands of soldiers needed to begin pushing the Nazis out of France and ultimately to topple Hitler and the Third Reich. Without the establishment of a beachhead there could be no ultimate victory. Establishing the beachhead was costly and bloody but it changed the course of human history. Within five days 326,547 troops, 54,186 vehicles, and 104,428 tons of supplies had flooded onto the shores of France. By June 30, just twenty four days after the initial beachhead, over 850,000 men, 148,000 vehicles, and 570,000 tons of supplies had arrived in France. This invasion was the decisive victory that turned the tide on World War II.

The washing and regeneration of the human spirit is the beachhead that God needed to establish within the hearts of His people in order to transform them from the inside out. It is the foundation from which He begins the mopping up operation of the ongoing sanctification of the soul. Everything that is true of Christ (apart from His Deity) is now true of us as a result of the miracle of regeneration. John said, "As He is, so are we in this world" (1 John 4:17). The first thing to note is that we have the same standing before the Father as Jesus has eternally enjoyed in His Father's presence. The key to this right standing is the free gift of righteousness, which we shall explore in the next chapter.

Chapter Eight

The Free Gift of Righteousness

What does it mean to have been made righteous in the sight of God? Ever since the fall, back in the Garden of Eden, the world has been filled with unrighteousness and ungodliness. It is part of the very atmosphere we breathe. Every single soul has become unrighteous in God's sight: "As it is written: 'There is none righteous, no, not one!'" (Romans 3:10). Unrighteousness is the absence or loss of a condition called righteousness. John said, "All unrighteousness is sin" (1 John 5:17). Paul charted humanity's descent into sin and darkness when he said, "Even as they did not like to retain God in their knowledge, God gave them over to a debased mind, to do those things which are not fitting; being filled with all unrighteousness" (Romans 1:28-29). Paul spoke of those who actually take "pleasure in unrighteousness" (2 Thessalonians 2:12). In stark contrast to this world of darkness and sin the Lord is gloriously righteous. Righteousness is one of the outstanding attributes of God.

> He is the Rock! His work is perfect for all His ways are just; a God of faithfulness and without injustice; righteous and upright is He." (Deuteronomy 32:4)

The Lord is righteous; He is my rock and there is no unrighteousness in Him. (Psalm 92:15)

What exactly is righteousness? It's important that we understand this concept because God has made us righteous in His sight through the new birth. The revelation of the free gift of righteousness is designed to fundamentally revolutionise our understanding of who we have become in the sight of God. Righteousness is the state of "being right." Dictionaries define righteous as "morally upright; without guilt or sin." In reference to God, it describes His uprightness, His divine nature, and His moral character. In reference to man it is spoken of as the impartation of the very divine nature of God. Peter said that regenerated Christians have become partakers of the divine nature. He begins his second epistle by extolling the reality that those who have faith have received the free gift of righteousness. He addresses his epistle to:

Those who through the righteousness of our God and Saviour Jesus Christ have received a faith as precious as ours: Grace and peace be yours in abundance through the knowledge of God and of Jesus our Lord. His divine power has given us everything we need for life and godliness through our knowledge of Him who called us by His own glory and goodness. Through these He has given us His very great and precious promises, so that through them you may participate in the divine nature and escape the corruption in the world caused by evil desires. (2 Peter 1:1-4 NIV)

The divine nature of God is defined by this term "righteousness." The only way God could reconcile the unrighteous and bring them back into intimate fellowship with Himself was to impart to fallen men and women the free gift of His own righteousness. "For what fellowship has righteousness with unrighteousness?" (2 Corinthians 6:14 KJV). God outlined His glorious New Covenant plan of salvation through the Old Testament prophets and announced His plan to clothe those who believe in Him with a robe of divine righteousness. "In His days Judah will be saved and Israel will dwell safely; now this is His name by which He will be called: The Lord our Righteousness" (Jeremiah 23:6). There was only one solution to the problem of human unrighteousness: God had to impart His own righteousness in order to redeem us so that we could come into right standing before Him.

> I will greatly rejoice in the Lord, my soul shall be joyful in my God; for He has clothed me with the garments of salvation, He has covered me with the robe of righteousness, as a Bridegroom decks himself with ornaments and as a bride adorns herself with her jewels. For as the earth brings forth its bud, as the garden causes the things that are sown in it to spring forth, so the Lord God will cause righteousness and praise to spring forth before all the nations. For Zion's sake I will not hold My peace and for Jerusalem's sake I will not rest, until her righteousness goes forth as brightness and her salvation as a lamp that burns. The Gentiles shall see your righteousness and all kings your glory. You shall be called by a new name, which the mouth of the Lord will name. You shall also be a crown of glory in the hand of the Lord and a royal diadem in the hand of your God. (Isaiah 60:10 – 62:3)

Righteousness springs forth in the earth through the free gift of the righteousness of Christ in human hearts. Jesus Christ is entirely righteous before the Father. One of His names is "Jesus Christ the righteous" (1 John 2:1). Concerning Himself, Jesus said, "He who speaks from himself seeks his own glory; but He who is seeking the glory of the One who sent Him, He is true, and there is no unrighteousness in Him" (John 7:18). Through this statement Jesus acknowledged His own deity or divine nature by echoing an exact phrase from the Old Testament about the righteousness of God. "The Lord is righteous; He is my rock, and there is no unrighteousness in Him" (Psalm 92:15). Those who believe in God are given the free gift of the righteousness of Christ as God imparts His own divine nature to their human spirit.

> For if, by the trespass of the one man, death reigned through that one man, how much more will those who receive God's abundant provision of grace and of the gift of righteousness reign in life through the one man, Jesus Christ. Consequently, just as the result of one trespass was condemnation for all men, so also the result of one act of righteousness was justification that brings life for all men. (Romans 5:17-18)

Paul's theology of the righteousness that comes by faith hinges on this act of divine justification. Justification by faith is inextricably interwoven with the free gift of righteousness. In order to see this clearly, we need to digress into a short Greek word study. There is a whole family of Greek words that all stem from one root word: *dikaios,* which means "morally upright, innocent, holy, without sin, blameless and *righteous.* This root word is translated in the New Testament as righteous and it is exclusively a descriptor of the divine nature of God. Righteous is an adjective which is a descriptive word. The noun form of *dikaios* is *dikaiosune,* which is translated as *righteousness.* A noun is the name of a person, place, or thing; therefore, righteousness is something that is a unique characteristic of God.

Now this is where our little word study gets really interesting. The verb form of righteous is *dikaioo,* which is translated into the English word *justify,* which means to "make righteous." Similarly, justification in Greek is *dikaiosis.* A verb is an action word, so to justify someone means to make them justified before God so that they begin to enjoy living in a state of complete justification before God. Justification is not something we can do for ourselves before God, even though we continually try to justify ourselves and our actions. Self-justification is nothing more than an assertion of self-righteousness. "All of us have become like one who is unclean, and all our righteous acts are like filthy rags" (Isaiah 64:6 NIV). In light of our Greek word study, thoughtfully consider the following passage from Romans 3. When I first saw this pattern I was greatly rewarded!

> But now a righteousness [*dikaiosune*] from God, apart from law, has been made known, to which the Law and the Prophets testify. This righteousness [*dikaiosune*] from God comes through faith in Jesus Christ to all who believe. There is no difference, for all have sinned and fall short of the glory of God, and are justified [*dikaioo*] freely by his grace through the redemption that came by Christ Jesus. God presented Him as a sacrifice of atonement, through faith in His blood. He did this to demonstrate His justice [*dikaiosune*], because in his forbearance he had left the sins committed beforehand unpunished – He did it to demonstrate His justice [*dikaiosune*] at the present time, so as to be just [*dikaios*] and the one who justifies [*dikaioo*] those who have faith in Jesus. (Romans 3:21-26 NIV)

The law was never given as a means to make us righteous in the sight of God. There are none righteous, not even those who strive to live a perfect life through keeping the law. Righteousness or justification cannot be earned or established through good works or human effort. It can only be bestowed upon us by God as He imparts the free gift of His own righteousness to us. Paul said, "But now the righteousness of God apart from the law is revealed, being witnessed by the Law and the Prophets" (Romans 3:21). The New Living Translation says, "But now God has shown us a different way of being right in his sight – not by obeying the law but by the way promised in the Scriptures long ago." This was through Jesus becoming our righteousness. "Now this is His name by which He will be called: The Lord our Righteousness" (Jeremiah 23:6).

Even Isaiah 53, that great chapter which details the atoning sacrifice of Christ, reveals that it is through the atonement that God has made a way through which He might justify those who believe in Him.

> He was oppressed and afflicted, yet He did not open His mouth; He was led like a lamb to the slaughter and as a sheep before her shearers is silent, so He did not open His mouth. By oppression and judgment He was taken away. And who can speak of His descendants? For He was cut off from the land of the living; for the transgression of My people He was stricken. He was assigned a grave with the wicked and with the rich in His death, though He had done no violence, nor was any deceit in His mouth. Yet it was the Lord's will to crush Him and cause Him to suffer, and though the Lord makes His life a guilt offering, He will see His offspring and prolong His days, and the pleasure of the Lord will prosper in His hand. After the suffering of His soul, He will see the light of life and be satisfied; by His knowledge My Righteous Servant will justify many, and He will bear their iniquities. Therefore I will give Him a portion among the great, and He will divide the spoils with the strong, because He poured out His life unto death, and was numbered with the transgressors. For He bore the sin of many, and made intercession for the transgressors. (Isaiah 53:7-12)

These are profound words: "My Righteous Servant will justify many!" The Hebrew word for righteous is *tsaddiyq*. The Hebrew word for justify is *tsadaq*, which means "to make righteous." *My Righteous Servant will make many righteous*. The good news is that God does not just declare us righteous, He actually makes us righteous! He has indeed declared us to be righteous, but He declares us righteous because He has made us righteous. "For He made Him who knew no sin to be sin for us, that we might become the righteousness of God in Him" (2 Corinthians 5:21). This is not theological hair-splitting. Some argue that God declares us positionally righteous by virtue of our faith. But God does way more than merely declaring us to be righteous. He makes us the righteousness of God in Christ. Wow!

Paul said, "It is because of him that you are in Christ Jesus, who has become for us wisdom from God – that is, our righteousness, holiness and redemption" (1 Corinthians 1:30 NIV). Jesus is the Lord our righteousness. Through the act of justification God does infinitely more that merely declaring us righteous (as though this was a theoretical state) in spite of the fact that we are still fundamentally sinners. No, God goes all the way by cleansing and washing your human spirit from all unrighteousness and by making your spirit just as righteous as Jesus Himself is righteous. Paul puts it this way: "If Christ is in you ... your spirit is alive because of righteousness" (Romans 8:10 NIV).

It is the free gift of righteousness that makes us alive to God. Sin brings death, but righteousness brings life. "Just as the result of one trespass was condemnation for all men, so also the result of one act of righteousness was *justification that brings life* for all men" (Romans 5:18 NIV). Our human spirit is now gloriously alive to God, exclusively because of the free gift of God's own righteousness. "So just as sin ruled over all people and brought them to death, now God's wonderful kindness rules instead, giving us right standing with God and *resulting in eternal life* through Jesus Christ our Lord" (Romans 5:21 NLT). "For the wages of sin is death, but the gift of God is eternal life in Christ Jesus our Lord" (Romans 6:23).

In his first epistle the Apostle John says, "My little children, these things I write to you, so that you may not sin. And if anyone sins, we have an Advocate with the Father, Jesus Christ the righteous" (1 John 2:1). In what way does Jesus become our Advocate? He acts as our advocate before the Father by becoming our righteousness. Later in the same chapter, John says, "If you know that He is righteous, you know that everyone who practices righteousness is born of Him" (1 John 2:29). "Little children, let no one deceive you. He who practices righteousness is righteous, just as He is righteous" (1 John 3:7).

Jesus is our Advocate even when we sin because He has imparted His divine nature of righteousness to our spirit. We are now justified before the Father to the same extent that Jesus is. We are justified, just as if we had never sinned. We are now righteous just as He is righteous. "Because as He is, so are we in this world" (1 John 4:17).

Jesus lived in a comprehensively justified state before the Father. "And without controversy great is the mystery of godliness: God was manifested in the flesh, *justified in the Spirit*, seen by angels, preached among the Gentiles, believed on in the world, received up in glory" (1 Timothy 3:16). The New Living Translation says, "Without question, this is the great mystery of our faith: Christ appeared in the flesh and was shown to be righteous by the Spirit. He was seen by angels and was announced to the nations. He was believed on in the world and was taken up into heaven." In the same way, we who have faith in Jesus are now shown to be righteous by the Spirit. We are also *justified in the Spirit* before the Father.

What a glorious life-transforming revelation. We have become the righteousness of God in Christ! This radically eclipses a mere declaration of righteousness as a temporal covering over unclean sinners. We are no longer sinners but saints in His sight because we have become righteous just as He is Righteous. This is our glorious standing before the Father. We have the same standing as Jesus has eternally enjoyed. We have free and unfettered access into an arena of spiritual blessedness that is so great that it boggles the mind.

What a glorious transaction. Jesus became sin and took the penalty of our sins by dying in our place on the cross in order that we might become righteous in our spirit. No wonder the Word of God separated the soul from the spirit, drawing a clear line of demarcation between the precious and the vile. "Therefore thus says the Lord: If you repent, then I will bring you back; you shall stand before Me; if you take out the precious from the vile you shall be as My mouth" (Jeremiah 15:19). What God has done in our spirit is inexpressibly precious. He has placed His very nature of righteousness in our human spirit so that we can be restored to right relationship with Him.

The book of Hebrews outlines the complete inability of the Old Covenant to make perfect the people of God. "For the law made nothing perfect [*teleioo*]; on the other hand, there is the bringing in of a better hope, through which we draw near to God" (Hebrews 7:19). This better hope is embodied in Jesus who ushered in a better covenant. "For the law, having a shadow of the good things to come, and not the very image of the things, can never with these same sacrifices, which they offer continually year by year, make those who approach perfect [*teleioo*]" (Hebrews 10:1). The writer of Hebrews repeatedly used this Greek word *teleioo* to describe a condition of spiritual completion.

His argument was that the law failed miserably to bring the people of God to this state of being complete before Him. The book of Hebrews juxtaposes the failure of the Old Covenant to complete the saints against the brilliant success of the New Covenant to achieve what the law could not do. "For by one offering He has perfected [teleioo] forever those who are being sanctified" (Hebrews 10:14). Only the atoning sacrifice of Jesus could achieve this work of bringing us to completion.

In Hebrews 12, the anonymous author contrasts Mount Sinai with Mount Zion. Mt. Sinai, of course, represents the giving of the law. He says, "You have not come to a mountain that can be touched and that is burning with fire; to darkness, gloom and storm; to a trumpet blast or to such a voice speaking words that those who heard it begged that no further word be spoken to them" (Hebrews 12:18-19 NIV). "But you have come to Mount Zion and to the city of the living God, the heavenly Jerusalem, to an innumerable company of angels, to the general assembly and church of the firstborn who are registered in heaven, to God the Judge of all, to the spirits of just men made perfect" (Hebrews 12:23). Here the writer brings into focus the miracle of the New Covenant. We who believe have become part of the church and we have come to the communion of saints, "...to the spirits of righteous [*dikaios*] men made perfect [*teleioo*]" (NIV).

The law could not make us righteous or bring us to completion. But now we have come to the general assembly and church of the firstborn who have been made righteous and who have already been brought to a state of spiritual completion. "If perfection [*teleioo*] could have been attained through the Levitical priesthood (for on the basis of it the law was given to the people), why was there still need for another priest to come?" (Hebrews 7:11). But "Christ came as High Priest of the good things that are already here" (Hebrews 9:11 NIV). He imparted His righteousness and brought our human spirit to a state of spiritual completion. Paul boldly declares, "You are *complete* in Him" (Colossians 2:10).

Your human spirit is so thoroughly immersed in Christ and the Holy Spirit that it is now pure, holy, righteous, completely free from sin, free from all guilt, blameless, washed, clean, justified, sanctified, and made perfectly right with God. Your human spirit is complete! This is the message of Hebrews and this is our new state of existence in the sight of God. We are invited to believe in the finished work of the Holy Spirit within our spirit, go into our inner room, and begin to enjoy the fullness that the Father has already poured out upon us. This new spiritual estate is so new and unfamiliar that it takes time for us to adjust to our new spiritual condition. We have been "called trees of righteousness, the planting of the Lord, that He may be glorified" (Isaiah 61:3). God continually speaks to the treasure within us. He calls out the treasure until we are so established in the finished work of Christ that it profoundly alters our entire self-perception and, subsequently, the way we live and carry ourselves in this world.

For Paul, justification by faith and the free gift of righteousness was much deeper than a profound theological revelation. It extended beyond a glorious biblical concept to a profound experiential reality.

This reality flowed out of an encounter with God. Through this encounter, God communicates to the human spirit what it means to be comprehensively right before Him, just as Jesus is right before the Father. Paul entered into the experience of being made entirely right before the Father so that peripheral realities did not shape his core identity. He was right with the Father based upon the finished work of Christ on the cross. Nothing could alter that reality because being justified or made righteous in the sight of God is also a finished work in the human spirit.

Ever since the reformation, theologians have marvelled at the glorious plan of salvation and the theology of justification by faith. But Paul lived beyond the theological description of this state. He had entered into the joy and peace of the free gift righteousness and he lived in the blessed estate of knowing he was completely right with God as a free gift. We must guard against the error of thinking that simply because we understand something theologically, we are automatically living in the rich experience of justification. Paul wrote his brilliant theology of Romans and Galatians out of his experience of absolute right standing before the Father. It would be his greatest sadness to see his readers get stuck in the theology of it all without experiencing the fruit of righteousness, which is glorious peace with God. "Therefore, having been justified by faith, we have peace with God through our Lord Jesus Christ" (Romans 5:1).

Chapter Nine

Partakers of the Divine Nature

"Grace and peace be multiplied to you in the knowledge of God and of Jesus our Lord, as His divine power has given to us all things that pertain to life and godliness, through the knowledge of Him who called us by glory and virtue, by which have been given to us exceedingly great and precious promises, that through these you may be *partakers of the divine nature*, having escaped the corruption that is in the world through lust." (2 Peter 1:2-4)

Every born again Christian has become a partaker of the divine nature of God in Christ. If you are born of the Spirit you have been given an entirely new nature in Christ. As part of the glorious package of the new creation miracle, God has imparted to our spirit a brand new nature. As we have seen repeatedly in all of the chapters of this book, your spirit has been supernaturally joined to the Lord. As a result of this mystical union, you are now in Christ. But greater than the fact that you are in Christ is the reality that Christ is in you. Christ, in the fullness of His glorious nature, has enfolded and encompassed your spirit and imparted His very nature to your spirit.

Paul extolled the endless virtues of "Christ in you, the hope of glory" Colossians 1:27). Christ Himself has become our confident expectation of the manifestation of the glory of God in and through our lives. Paul said, "Examine yourselves to see whether you are in the faith; test yourselves. Do you not realize that Christ Jesus is in you – unless, of course, you fail the test?" (2 Corinthians 13:5 NIV). Christ is our new life. "When Christ, *who is our life*, is revealed, then you also will be revealed with Him in glory" (Colossians 3:4). Your life has now been infused with His life and we now live "according to the power of an endless life" (Hebrews 7:16).

Peter said, "His divine power has given to us all things that pertain to *life* and godliness." This "life" is the *zoe* life of God Himself that has been imparted to your spirit to make your spirit come alive. As we saw in chapter three, your old sinful nature has been circumcised or cut away. God has joined these two extremely powerful realities together in His Word to magnify the glory of the new creation. Your old sinful nature has been surgically cut away and you are now a partaker of the divine nature. Let's read again what Paul said about the circumcision of the heart:

> When you came to Christ, you were "circumcised," but not by a physical procedure. It was a spiritual procedure – *the cutting away of your sinful nature*. For you were buried with Christ when you were baptized. And with him you were raised to a new life because you trusted the mighty power of God, who raised Christ from the dead. You were dead because of your sins and because *your sinful nature was not yet cut away*. Then God made you alive with Christ. He forgave all our sins. He cancelled the record that contained the charges against us. He took it and destroyed it by nailing it to Christ's cross. (Colossians 2:11-14 NLT)

God has cut away the old sinful nature from your spirit and has replaced it with the new divine nature of Christ. This means that the very nature of Christ becomes our glorious new nature. It has been imparted to our spirit so that we become partakers. The Greek word Peter used for this reality is *koinonos,* which means to share something in common. If we have an entry level knowledge of some of the most famous Greek words of the New Testament, we will recognise that this is a cognate of the Greek word *koinonia,* which means fellowship or communion that flows out of a common union. It means oneness. Paul said that those who are joined to the Lord have become one spirit with Him, our spirit encased by His Spirit in deep mystical union.

As a result of the circumcision of the heart, the cutting away of your sinful nature, Paul taught that those who have been born of God "do not live according to the sinful nature but according to the Spirit. Those who live according to the sinful nature have their minds set on what that nature desires; but those who live in accordance with the Spirit have their minds set on what the Spirit desires" (Romans 8:4-5). "But you are not in the flesh but in the Spirit, if indeed the Spirit of God dwells in you" (Romans 8:9). Because we are now "in the Spirit" we no longer live according to the sinful nature. We live according to the new nature of Christ in us. Your new nature gives you an entirely new desire to please God, to hate sin, and to love righteousness. It becomes unnatural to love sin because God robs us of taking any pleasure whatsoever in unrighteousness. Right after we are born again, we immediately feel within us the power of this new life and new nature.

Our responsibility is to put on the Lord Jesus Christ and His divine nature. "Put on the Lord Jesus Christ, and make no provision for the flesh, to fulfill its lusts" (Romans 13:14). "Rather, clothe yourselves with the Lord Jesus Christ, and do not think about how to gratify the desires of the sinful nature" (NIV). Our new self has been supernaturally created to be just like God in righteousness and holiness.

You were taught, with regard to your former way of life, to put off *your old self*, which is being corrupted by its deceitful desires; to be made new in the attitude of your minds; and to put on *the new self*, created to be like God in true righteousness and holiness. (Ephesians 4:22-24 NIV)

Your old self consisted in the old sinful nature, but your new self consists in the new divine nature of Christ. As a person who has been "born from above," God is continually calling out your new nature. He is no longer pastoring your old nature; He has put it to death. God now relates to you as a new creation with a new nature and He is constantly in dialogue with your new nature. Now, as we look within, we discover that our old sinful nature has been cut away and replaced by the divine nature of Christ. The miracle of the new creation is that Christ lives in us, as us. "It's no longer I who lives but Christ who lives in me."

The Christian life has now become an unfolding revelation of the divine nature in us. Misguided Christians who, with the best of intentions, say that you are nothing but a sinner saved by grace have completely missed the miracle that has already occurred. God isn't telling you that you are a sinner saved by grace; He is telling you that you are a saint who has been set free of his or her old sinful nature. He relentlessly calls out your new nature until you become gripped by this revelation.

What exactly is this divine nature that has already been communicated to our heart through the new birth? To contemplate the divine nature all we need to do is to behold the glory of the nature of Christ. A.W. Tozer once said, "What comes into our minds when we think about God is the most important thing about us." In his 1961 book, *The Knowledge of the Holy*, he wrote:

The message of this book ... is called forth by a condition which has existed in the Church for some years and is steadily growing worse. I refer to the loss of the concept of *majesty* from the popular Christian mind. The Church has surrendered her once lofty concept of God and has substituted it for one so low, so ignoble, as to be utterly unworthy of thinking, worshipping men. The low view of God entertained almost universally among Christians is the cause of a hundred lesser evils everywhere among us. With our loss of the sense of majesty has come the further loss of spiritual awe and consciousness of the divine Presence. We have lost our spirit of worship and our ability to withdraw inwardly to meet God in adoring silence.[11]

We are called to meditate upon the splendour and majesty of God. The Psalmist wrote, "I will meditate on the glorious splendor of Your majesty and on Your wondrous works" (Psalm 145:5). Meditation upon the nature of God is central to our devotional life. Graham Cooke says, "Many people's image of God is flawed – yet what we think about God is the single most important thing in our spiritual journey."[12] Meditating upon the multifaceted majesty of God is the best way to explore the scope and breadth of the divine nature. As we meditate upon the glory of God, we are drawn into the ultimate mystery. According to Paul, Christ in us is the mystery that has been kept hidden from ages past but is now being revealed prophetically to the saints. This mystery is now being revealed to the glorious sons and daughters of God (Colossians 1:26-27).

God's Own Nature is Communicable

The Bible distinguishes between the communicable and non-communicable attributes of the nature of God. Certain aspects of the nature of God are effectively incommunicable, meaning that God never communicates these attributes to His sons and daughters. These are attributes of the nature of God that belong exclusively to the triune Godhead.

- God is uncreated (He has no first cause)
- God is eternal (He is without beginning or end)
- God is infinite (He knows no limitation)
- God is self-existent (He is entirely independent)
- God is transcendent (He transcends everything)
- God is omniscient (He knows absolutely everything)
- God is omnipresent (He is present everywhere)
- God is omnipotent (He is all powerful)
- God is immutable (He does not and cannot change)

God's very nature is revealed in all of these attributes but none of them are communicable. However, every aspect of the moral nature and character of God is directly communicable through the new creation. The following 33 attributes of the nature of God are all communicated to the spirit of God's beloved sons and daughters.

God is Life

"He is the only true God, and He is eternal life." (1 John 5:20)

God is Light

"God is light and in Him is no darkness at all." (1 John 1:5)

God is True

"Though everyone else in the world is a liar, God is true." (Romans 3:4)

Jesus said, "I am the truth." (John 14:6)

God is Wise

"God is wise in heart and mighty in strength." (Job 9:4)

God is Powerful

"Great is our Lord, and mighty in power; His understanding is infinite." (Psalms 147:5)

God is Fire

"For the Lord your God is a consuming fire, a jealous God." (Deuteronomy 4:24)

God is Heart

"I have found David the son of Jesse, a man after My own heart, who will do all My will." (Acts 13:22)

God is Father

"Our Father who is in heaven…" (Matthew 6:9)

God is Heavenly

"My heavenly Father." (Matthew 18:35)

God is Glorious

"Our glorious Lord Jesus Christ." (James 2:1 NNAS)

"The God of our Lord Jesus Christ, the glorious Father." (Ephesians 1:17 NIV)

God is Majestic

"The Lord reigns, He is clothed with majesty." (Psalm 93:1)

"I will meditate on the glorious splendour of Your majesty." (Psalm 145:5)

God is Beautiful

"To behold the beauty of the Lord and to inquire in His temple." (Psalm 27:4)

God is Perfect

"Your Father in heaven is perfect." (Matthew 5:48)

God is Holy

"For the Lord our God is holy." (Psalms 99:9)

God is Pure

"Everyone who has this hope in Him purifies himself, just as He is pure." (1 John 3:3)

God is Righteous

"For the Lord our God is righteous." (Daniel 9:14)

God is Upright

"A God of truth and without injustice; righteous and upright is He." (Deuteronomy 32:4)

God is Just

"God is just." (2 Thessalonians 1:6 NIV)

"For the Lord is a God of justice." (Isaiah 30:18)

God is Zealous (Passionate)

"I, the Lord, have spoken it in My zeal." (Ezekiel 5:13)

"The passion of the Lord Almighty will make this happen!" (Isaiah 37:32 NLT)

God is Love

"For God is love." (1 John 4:8)

God is Peace

"Now the God of peace be with you all." (Romans 15:33)

God is Joy

"That they may have My joy fulfilled in themselves." (John 17:13)

"For the joy of the Lord is your strength." (Nehemiah 8:10)

God is Gentle

"For I am gentle and lowly in heart, and you will find rest for your souls." (Matthew 11:29)

God is Good

"Only God is good." (Matthew 19:17 NLT)

God is Kind

"The kindness and the love of God our Saviour." (Titus 3:4)

God is Gracious

"Gracious is the Lord, and righteous; Yes, our God is merciful." (Psalms 116:5)

God is Merciful

"The Lord God, merciful and gracious, longsuffering, and abounding in goodness and truth." (Exodus 34:6)

God is Compassionate

"You are a forgiving God, gracious and compassionate." (Nehemiah 9:17)

God is Faithful

"God is faithful." (1 Corinthians 1:9)

God is Patient

"The Lord is not slow about His promise, as some count slowness, but is patient toward you." (2 Peter 3:9 NAS)

God is Self Controlled

"The Lord is slow to anger and great in power." (Nahum 1:3)

God is Humble

"In Your majesty ride prosperously because of truth, humility, and righteousness." (Psalms 45:4)

"Let me teach you, because I am humble and gentle." (Matthew 11:29 NLT)

The Communication of the Divine Nature

God is infinite in all of the characteristics of His divine nature; however, these can only be finitely communicated in a limited sense. Even when these divine attributes are communicated to the hearts of God's sons and daughters, these attributes always remain His attributes. Nevertheless, God is gracious in His intent to make us *finite partakers of His infinite and perfect divine nature*. The fruits of the Holy Spirit, listed in Galatians 5, are communicable so that we are enabled to partake of the nature of God. "The fruit of the Spirit is love, joy, peace, patience, kindness, goodness, faithfulness, gentleness and self-control" (Galatians 5:22-23 NIV). Of course, the nine fruits listed in this passage are not definitive. Paul lists other fruits in other places in the body of his writings. "For you were once darkness, but now you are light in the Lord. Walk as children of light (for the fruit of the Spirit is in all goodness, righteousness, and truth)" (Ephesians 5:8-9).

Therefore, as God's chosen people, holy and dearly loved, clothe yourselves with compassion, kindness, humility, gentleness and patience. Bear with each other and forgive whatever grievances you may have against one another. Forgive as the Lord forgave you. And over all these virtues put on love, which binds them all together in perfect unity. (Colossians 3:12-14 NIV) Pursue a godly life, along with faith, love, perseverance, and gentleness." (1 Timothy 6:11 NLT)

God communicates the fullness of His life, His glory, and His virtues to all of His sons and daughters. In fact, the term "glory" is an umbrella term that encompasses every aspect of the divine nature. Glory is the family trait of the Father, the Son, the Holy Spirit, and His "whole family in heaven and earth" (Ephesians 3:15). "His divine power has given to us all things that pertain to life and godliness, through the knowledge of Him who called us by glory and virtue" (2 Peter 1:3). The New Living Translation says, "He has called us to receive his own glory and goodness." According to Paul, "He called you by our gospel, for the obtaining of the glory of our Lord Jesus Christ" (2 Thessalonians 2:14).

Beholding as in a Mirror

Paul taught that one of the greatest keys for our supernatural transformation, alongside the renewing of our minds, is in beholding the glory of God in the face of Christ. "But we all, with unveiled face, beholding as in a mirror the glory of the Lord, are being transformed into the same image from glory to glory, just as by the Spirit of the Lord" (2 Corinthians 3:18). This is the principle of **beholding and becoming.** It is only as we behold Him that we become like Him. No beholding results in no becoming! Beholding and gazing upon the glory of God in the face of Christ is the greatest key to our personal transformation. We learn from Moses' encounter with God that God's glory is most fully revealed through His nature.

> Moses said, "Please, show me Your glory." Then He said, "I will make all My goodness pass before you, and I will proclaim the name of the Lord before you." (Exodus 33:18,19)

Every attribute of God is resplendent in glory. To behold the glory of the Lord is to simultaneously behold the perfection of all of these attributes of the divine nature of God. The Greek word for "mirror" in 2 Corinthians 3:18 is **katoptrizomai**. It means "to gaze into a mirror, to see reflected, or to mirror oneself." The New Living Translation says, "And all of us have had that veil removed so that we can be mirrors that brightly reflect the glory of the Lord." As we behold the glory of the Lord, we mirror, or reflect, that glory because the glory of the Lord is in us by virtue of the new nature that was imparted when our spirit was washed and regenerated.

Worshipping God is therefore the key that releases glory. We must become worshippers in order to be transformed by His glory. Gazing upon the glory of the Lord unlocks powerful spiritual realities within us. Paul taught that beholding the very nature of God is the key to manifesting the divine nature. Deep calls out to deep. We become like the one we worship. As we behold the glory of God in the face of Christ, we discover who we now are as new creations. As we behold His wholeness, we experience healing in every area of our broken and shattered soul. We become increasingly whole, mentally and emotionally, as we gaze upon the glory of Christ.

God is most glorified in us as His divine nature is revealed in us. Throughout the New Testament we see the nature of God communicated to the hearts of His people in order that we may reflect His glory. It's extraordinary that God would choose to communicate so much of His glory to His sons and daughters. The theme of inheritance, most fully developed by Paul, revolves exclusively around the impartation of the riches of the glory of God to His very own people. In five separate places, Paul unpacks the relationship between the riches of our inheritance and the glory of God. These verses are Romans 9:23, Ephesians 1:18, 3:16, Philippians 4:19, and Colossians 1:27.

Earlier in this chapter we examined thirty-three attributes of the communicable nature of God. We now close this chapter by examining these same thirty-three attributes of the divine nature as they are revealed in reference to the life of the New Testament people of God.

The power of meditating upon these realities is in realising that the more we contemplate these things the more we will be empowered to manifest the divine nature through our lives, just as Jesus manifested the life of His Father when He was on earth. God really wants us to take a hold of the fact that we are now partakers of the divine nature through the miracle of the new creation.

God is Life

"He who has the Son has life; he who does not have the Son of God does not have life." (1 John 5:12)

God is Light

"For you were once darkness, but now you are light in the Lord." (Ephesians 5:8)

God is True

"By this we know that we are of the truth." (1 John 3:19)

God is Wise

"If any of you lacks wisdom, he should ask God, who gives generously to all." (James 1:5 NIV)

God is Powerful

"But truly I am full of power by the Spirit of the Lord." (Micah 3:8)

God is Fire

"He will baptize you with the Holy Spirit and fire." (Matthew 3:11)

God is Heart

"Doing the will of God from the heart." (Ephesians 6:6)

God is Father

"I write to you, fathers, because you have known Him who is from the beginning." (1 John 2:13)

God is Heavenly

"As is the heavenly Man, so also are those who are heavenly." (1 Corinthians 15:48)

God is Glorious

"He called you by our gospel for the obtaining of the glory of our Lord Jesus Christ." (2 Thessalonians 2:14)

God is Majestic

"His glory is great in Your salvation; honour and majesty You have placed upon him." (Psalms 21:5)

God is Beautiful

"Let the beauty of the Lord our God be upon us." (Psalms 90:17)

God is Perfect

"Therefore you shall be perfect, just as your Father in heaven is perfect." (Matthew 5:48)

God is Holy

"That we may be partakers of His holiness." (Hebrews 12:10)

God is Pure

"Blessed are the pure in heart for they shall see God." (Matthew 5:8)

God is Righteous

"That we might become the righteousness of God in Him." (2 Corinthians 5:21)

God is Upright

"The righteous shall be glad in the Lord, and trust in Him. And all the upright in heart shall glory." (Psalms 64:10)

God is Just

"But the path of the just is like the shining sun that shines ever brighter unto the perfect day." (Proverbs 4:18)

God is Zealous (Passionate)

"That He might purify for Himself His own special people, zealous for good works." (Titus 2:14)

God is Love

"May the Lord make you increase and abound in love to one another and to all." (1 Thessalonians 3:12)

God is Peace

"Now may the God of hope fill you with all joy and peace in believing." (Romans 15:13)

God is Joy

"Gladness and joy will overtake them, and sorrow and sighing will flee away." (Isaiah 35:10 NIV)

God is Gentle

"Let your gentleness be known to all men." (Philippians 4:5)

God is Good

"Now I myself am confident concerning you, my brethren, that you also are full of goodness." (Romans 15:14)

God is Kind

"Therefore, as the elect of God, holy and beloved, put on tender mercies, kindness, humility, meekness, longsuffering." (Colossians 3:12)

God is Gracious

"Let your conversation be gracious and effective."
(Colossians 4:6 NLT)

God is Merciful

"Therefore be merciful, just as your Father also is merciful."
(Luke 6:36)

God is Compassionate

"Be sympathetic, love as brothers, be compassionate and humble." (1 Peter 3:8 NIV)

God is Faithful

"Those who are with Him are called, chosen, and faithful."
(Revelation 17:14)

God is Patient

"Encourage the timid, help the weak, be patient with everyone."
(1 Thessalonians 5:14)

God is Self-controlled

"Be self-controlled and alert." (1 Peter 5:8 NIV)

God is Humble

"Be clothed with humility, for "God resists the proud but gives grace to the humble." (1 Peter 5:5)

As a concluding word on this subject, we come back to Peter's amazing passage where he proclaimed that *"you may be partakers of the divine nature,* having escaped the corruption that is in the world through lust" (2 Peter 1:4). Peter taught that the key to escaping the corruption of the lusts of the flesh is in partaking, by faith, in the glorious divine nature of Christ that has been transferred to our hearts through the new birth. This is the New Testament principle of displacement so clearly articulated by Paul when he said, "Put on the Lord Jesus Christ, and make no provision for the flesh, to fulfill its lusts" (Romans 13:14).

Putting on Christ in the fullness of His divine nature is clearly the most powerful way of breaking the shackles of lust rather than relentlessly seeking to combat lust as a strategy to overcome the old sinful nature. The devil loves to draw us into a battle with the fruits of the flesh without any consideration of the impartation of the new divine nature of Christ. Clearly the revelation of the gift of the new divine nature is a foundational key to overcoming everything that constituted our old life. Paul taught that we conquer evil with good!

Chapter Ten

Fully Immersed in the Spirit of Christ

The foundation of the personal transformation of our hearts begins with a revelatory knowledge of what God has already done in our human spirit. Without the establishment of this firm foundation, we will constantly revert to a model of change that is rooted in an attempt to conform to outward rules and regulations, instead of an expression of change and transformation, which springs from the inside out as a work of the Spirit. Paul said in Romans that we are transformed by the renewing of our minds. This profound mind renewal flows out of the revelation of the new creation.

The purpose of this chapter is twofold: to deepen our understanding of the work of the Spirit in our lives and to understand the fact that our human spirit is now permanently located in heaven. Through the new birth we have collectively become a company of heavenly men and women who are citizens of heaven, seated in heavenly places in Christ.

So it is written: "The first man Adam became a living being;" the last Adam, a life-giving spirit. The spiritual did not come first, but the natural, and after that the spiritual. The first man was of the dust of the earth, the second Man from heaven. As was the earthly man, so are those who are of the earth; and as is the Man from heaven, so also are those who are of heaven. And just as we have borne the likeness of the earthly man, so shall we bear the likeness of the Man from heaven. (1 Corinthians 15:45-49 NIV)

Our human spirit has now entered into the same status, or standing, before the Father as the human spirit of Jesus the man when He walked upon the earth. It has been renewed so that it is comprehensively new. There are two primary Greek words for "new." The first word is *neos,* which means new in respect to time, as in a new day. The second word is *kainos,* which means new in respect to quality or kind. A new [kainos] creation is comprehensively new in kind: it is something that has never been seen before. It is of an entirely different order of existence because it resembles the very life of Christ. When Paul spoke about the renewing of the Holy Spirit in Titus 3:5 he used the word *anakainosis,* which is derived from the Greek work *kainos.*

"We were therefore buried with him through baptism into death in order that, just as Christ was raised from the dead through the glory of the Father, we too may live a new life [*kainos*]" (Romans 6:4 NIV). When Jesus was on earth, He was the "Heavenly Man." He was the man who came down from heaven! "No one has ascended to heaven but He who came down from heaven, that is, the Son of Man who is in heaven" (John 3:13). Paul made the extraordinary statement that we are also now heavenly men and women because we are part of this glorious new [*kainos*] creation. Jesus is "the firstborn among many brethren" (Romans 8:29).

We have been so profoundly and comprehensively changed and renewed that we do not yet know our own true selves. Paul said, "Examine yourselves as to whether you are in the faith. Test yourselves. Do you not know yourselves that Jesus Christ is in you?" (2 Corinthians 13:5). Ask yourself this question: Do you really know yourself as a new creation? Paul said to test yourselves [*dokimazo*], which really means to "discern yourselves" in the light of the miracle of regeneration. Paul said, "Therefore, from now on, we regard no one according to the flesh" (2 Corinthians 5:16). Instead, we are now under obligation to know ourselves and one another according to the revelation of the new creation. This revelation begins with the recognition that we have been fundamentally changed on the inside and that we are in no way the same as we were before the new birth. "For as in Adam all die, even so in Christ all shall be made alive" (1 Corinthians 15:22).

God could not place an unregenerate, sinful spirit in His Beloved Son, so first He had to make your spirit completely new [*kainos*] before He could immerse you into the person of His Son. We really need to understand by revelation that our spirit is now fully immersed in Christ, so much so that we are no longer in the flesh, we are now in the Spirit. Your new place of residence is IN the very Spirit of Christ. "You are not in the flesh but in the Spirit, if indeed the Spirit of God dwells in you" (Romans 8:9). Paul asked, "Are you so foolish? Having begun in the Spirit, are you now being made perfect by the flesh?" (Galatians 3:3).

You began your Christian life in the Spirit. From the moment of the new birth God sees you no longer as being "in the flesh" but "in the Spirit." Never mind how you perceived yourself the moment you were born again. It is how God sees you that matters, because He has purposed that through the Spirit of revelation you will eventually begin to see yourself through His eyes. As a result, you will inevitably see yourself as an entirely new creation in Christ. Faith gives us the capacity to behold unseen things.

In Christ

This concept of being in Christ is the central pillar of Pauline theology. We have been "created in Christ Jesus" (Ephesians 2:10). Paul used the term "in Christ" eighty-five times in the NKJV. God is seeking to bring us into a place where we see our spirit as fully immersed into the person of Christ. The Holy Spirit is the Spirit of revelation who opens our eyes to heavenly realities. Jesus promised that the Holy Spirit would usher us into a place of spiritual vision where we would come to a clear comprehension of the reality that we are now in Christ. "And I will ask the Father, and He will give you another Counsellor to be with you forever – the Spirit of Truth. On that day you will realize that I am in My Father, and you are in Me, and I am in you" (John 14:16, 17, 20 NIV). God is seeking to unveil a twofold revelation: the revelation of Christ in you and the revelation of you in Christ. We are now "in Christ" in exactly the same way that Jesus is "in the Father." Jesus promised that the day would come when we would realize it!

Paul gloried in this twofold revelation. He diligently sought to bring everyone under His pastoral care into a place of prophetic clarity concerning the revelation that Jesus promised would come through the ministry of the Holy Spirit. Paul taught that every believer has been baptized into Christ. He had such a clear God-given vision of the spirit of every believer having been fully immersed into Christ that he laboured in prayer and in preaching to present every man perfect in Christ. "We proclaim Him, admonishing and teaching everyone with all wisdom, so that we may present everyone perfect in Christ. To this end I labour, struggling with all His energy, which so powerfully works in me" (Colossians 1:28-29). Some translations use the term "complete in Christ" rather than "perfect" because we are brought to a place of completion [*teleios*] in our relationship with the Father, the Son, and the Holy Spirit through the new birth.

Baptized into Christ

Romans chapter 6 is a profound and unparalleled revelation of the new creation. It is Paul's theological and revelatory epiphany that he sought to establish in the heart of every believer. It is also an extraordinary prophetic declaration of the reality of the new creation.

> Do you not know that as many of us as were baptized into Christ Jesus were baptized into His death? Therefore we were buried with Him through baptism into death, that just as Christ was raised from the dead by the glory of the Father, even so we also should walk in newness of life. (Romans 6:3-4)

Paul is not talking about water baptism in Romans 6. He is describing the dynamics of the new creation miracle in the heart of every believer. Our spirits have been gloriously baptized into Christ. "For as many of you as were baptized into Christ have put on Christ" (Galatians 3:27). The Greek word "baptized" [*baptizo*] means to be fully immersed or placed into an entirely new medium or reality. Baptism into water means to be placed or immersed into a body of water. In like manner, baptism into Christ means to be immersed into a person. Remember, Jesus promised that when He – the Spirit of Truth – comes, He will usher you into the revelation that "you are in Me, and I am in you" (John 14:20). We have been fully immersed into the triune Godhead. Christ is in the Father so if you are in Christ, you are also automatically in the Father. Jesus prayed "that they all may be one, as You, Father, are in Me, and I in You; that they also may be one in Us, that the world may believe that You sent Me" (John 17:21).

Spirit Baptism

Paul taught that just as we are "in Christ" so we are also "in the Spirit." He taught that every believer begins the Christian life in the Spirit from day one (Galatians 3:3). Because we have begun our Christian walk in the Spirit, there is an imperative to learn how to live and walk in the Spirit. "If we live in the Spirit, let us also walk in the Spirit" (Galatians 5:25). To Paul there was no difference between being baptized into Christ and being baptized into the Spirit. In Pauline theology it is all the same thing. Paul's theology radically critiques all "two-stage initiation" theologies that seek to outline a two-step program of initiation into the fullness of the Spirit. I have searched Paul's theology for over three decades and I am confident that Paul did not teach anything akin to current Pentecostal theology, which distinguishes the baptism in the Spirit from baptism into Christ. On the contrary, Paul taught a simple one-step model of initiation into life in the Spirit. He taught that there was one Lord, one Spirit, and one baptism.

> There is one body and one Spirit, just as you were called in one hope of your calling; one Lord, one faith, one baptism; one God and Father of all, who is above all, and through all, and in you all. (Ephesians 4:4-6)

Paul deliberately sought to undermine any theology that had the potential to carry Christians away into erroneous views concerning the believer's immersion into the Holy Spirit. The early Gnostics who emerged within the church at Corinth were seeking to establish a two-stage initiation theology, which divided the saints into two classes: the *psuchikos* and the *pneumatikos*. The Gnostic believers perceived themselves as *pneumatikos* or "spiritual" [from the Greek word *pneuma*, which means spirit], claiming that they had a special relationship to the Holy Spirit. They exalted themselves over the *psuchikos* [meaning soulish or natural] believers, who they looked down upon as inferior Christians. In order to prove their deeper spirituality, the *pneumatikos* displayed their superiority by speaking continually in tongues. Paul had to correct this error by addressing the appropriate use of tongues in the Corinthian church so that no one was made to feel inferior, especially those who did not possess the gift. New Testament commentators universally recognise that this was the background to the first epistle to the Corinthians.

Paul countered this dangerous drift toward a two class mentality by affirming the universality of the gift of the Spirit amongst New-Testament believers. According to Paul, a person either has the Spirit or they do not have the Spirit; if they have the gift of the Spirit, then-they have already been immersed "in the Spirit." "You, however, are controlled not by the sinful nature but by the Spirit, if the Spirit of God lives in you. And if anyone does not have the Spirit of Christ, he does not belong to Christ" (Romans 8:9). All believers have the gift of the Spirit. This was confirmed by Peter who was recorded in Acts as saying, "Repent, and let every one of you be baptized in the name of Jesus Christ for the remission of sins; and you shall receive the gift of the Holy Spirit" (Acts 2:38).

Paul taught that we have all been baptized in one Spirit, into one body, and have all been made to drink of one Spirit. Paul made this prophetic declaration to the Corinthians because they were beginning to fall into the error of a two-class system with a two-stage initiation. He said, "For we were all baptized by one Spirit into one body – whether Jews or Greeks, slave or free – and we were all given the one Spirit to drink" (1 Corinthians 12:13 NIV).

Gordon Fee, one of the most highly respected Pentecostal theologians of the twenty-first century, is widely recognized as one of the world's leading authorities on Pauline pneumatology.[13] He translates this passage in this way: "For indeed, we were all baptized in one Spirit so as to form one body, whether Jews or Greeks, slave or free and we were all given one Spirit to drink to the fill."

The critical issue in this passage is the Greek preposition *en* that Paul uses. He said, "We were all baptized in [en] one Spirit." Fee points out that the Greek preposition *en* is variously translated: "in, with, or by." In this passage, the Spirit is the element into which the Corinthians were all baptized. Fee and many other evangelical scholars believe that Paul deliberately wrote this passage to highlight the fact that all believers have been immersed into the person of the Holy

Spirit. The one Spirit/one body motif undermines any drift toward a two-stage initiation that was clearly beginning to take place in the Corinthian church. This is Paul's one and only specific reference to any concept of Spirit baptism in his entire body of work[14] and his clear agenda is to emphasise the unity of the body of Christ as joint heirs of the gift of the Holy Spirit.

Any movement toward a two-stage initiation inevitably creates "superior" and "inferior" believers: those who have the Spirit in His fullness and those who somehow come up short. Paul would be mortified to witness some of our popular contemporary pneumatologies, which inadvertently create a definite two class system consisting of those with an "ordinary" relationship to the Spirit and those with a "special" relationship to the Spirit. This line of thinking is diametrically opposed to Paul's theology that there is one body and one Spirit of which we have all been given the privilege to drink or partake. Paul boldly asserts, "We were all given one Spirit to drink in fullness!" It is noteworthy that this concept in 1 Corinthians 12:13 is similarly reflected throughout Paul's entire theology of the Spirit and his teaching on the unity of the Spirit in the body of Christ.

There is also no question that Paul equated the outpouring of the Holy Spirit with the new birth. "He saved us through the washing of rebirth and renewal by the Holy Spirit, whom He poured out on us generously through Jesus Christ our Savior, so that, having been justified by His grace, we might become heirs having the hope of eternal life" (Titus 3:5-7 NIV). In Paul's theology the rebirth of the Spirit is synonymous with the outpouring of the Holy Spirit. This idea is echoed in Romans 5, "Therefore, since we have been justified through faith, we have peace with God through our Lord Jesus Christ, through whom we have gained access by faith into this grace in which we now stand ... because God has *poured out* His love into our hearts by the Holy Spirit, whom He has given us" (Romans 5:1-5 NIV).

When we receive the Holy Spirit at conversion we receive all of Him, not just part of Him. The Holy Spirit is a person. Whenever God gives the gift of the Spirit, He is always *poured out in fullness.* "The Jewish believers who came with Peter were amazed that the gift of the Holy Spirit had been poured out upon the Gentiles too" (Acts 10:45). In Paul's theology the initial reception (or gift) of the Spirit is unquestionably equated with the outpouring of the Holy Spirit. How do we receive *part* of a person? Did you receive part of Christ at conversion? Were you partly immersed into Christ or were you fully immersed into the fullness of Christ when you first believed? Were you partly immersed in the Spirit at conversion or were you fully immersed into the person of the Spirit? Paul taught that we have either received the gift of the outpouring of the Holy Spirit or we have not! Interestingly, the Gospel of John would appear to support the idea that when we receive the gift of the Holy Spirit we receive all of Him in His fullness.

Filled with the Spirit

John the Baptist boldly proclaimed that "God does not give His Spirit by measure" (John 3:34). The word "measure" is *metron* in Greek and it means "by degree or by limited portion." Therefore, the NIV says, "For God gives the Spirit without limit." The Amplified Bible says, "God does not give His Spirit sparingly or by measure, but boundless is the gift God makes of His Spirit." The Message Bible says, "Don't think He (God) rations out the Spirit in bits and pieces!" Holy Spirit is a person, He is not a substance or a commodity. If we *receive the Spirit,* we receive Him as a person in His fullness. There is an impartation of the fullness of the Spirit of God to every born again believer, just as there is an impartation of the fullness of the person of Christ to every believer.

The Apostle John said, "Of His fullness we have all received and grace for grace" (John 1:16). In like manner Paul said, "For in Christ all the fullness of the Deity lives in bodily form, and you have been given fullness in Christ" (Colossians 2:9-10 NIV). This fullness obviously includes the fullness of the Holy Spirit. We can emphatically conclude that when God gives the gift of His Spirit, He pours Him out upon us in fullness.

At issue, of course, is our capacity to walk in the fullness of the Spirit. Our problem is that we leak! We are leaky and broken vessels. Who except for Jesus can walk in the absolute fullness of the Spirit anyway? That is why Paul highlighted the necessity of frequent infillings with the Holy Spirit: "Do not get drunk on wine, which leads to debauchery. Instead, be filled with the Spirit" (Ephesians 4:18). The Greek tense of this verb is "Be being filled...." Paul exhorted us to be continuously filled with the Spirit. The Message Bible says, "Don't drink too much wine. Drink the Spirit of God: huge draughts of Him!"

Even in the book of Acts there was the initial filling up of the Holy Spirit followed by subsequent infillings. "All of them were filled with the Holy Spirit and began to speak in other tongues as the Spirit enabled them" (Acts 2:4). But then, just two chapters later we read: "After they prayed, the place where they were meeting was shaken. And they were all filled with the Holy Spirit and spoke the word of God boldly" (Acts 4:31).

Paul's vision for believers was that they could be brought to the place where they could live experientially in the fullness of the Spirit's presence and power. He prayed, "That you may be filled to the measure of all the fullness of God" (Ephesians 3:19). In effect Paul was praying, "That you may be experientially filled to the measure of all the fullness of the Spirit of God." So how do we reconcile the idea that we have been given the gift of the Holy Spirit in His fullness yet we are exhorted to be continually filled with the Spirit? The answer lies once again in the discussion in previous chapters where Paul differentiated between the soul and the spirit. It is your spirit that has been gloriously baptized, or immersed into, the fullness of Christ and the Spirit. Your spirit is permanently Spirit-filled! The work of God in your human spirit is a finished work that cannot be added to or upgraded. But in contrast, the work of God in your soul is a definite work in progress. It is an unfinished work. Paul said, "Being confident of this very thing; that He who has begun a good work in you will complete it" (Philippians 1:6).

The reality of the clear biblical differentiation between the soul and the spirit sheds a great deal of light upon the ongoing work of the Spirit. In particular, the work the Spirit does in bringing every area of our un-renewed soul under the rule and reign of the Holy Spirit, who is gloriously united to our human spirit. There is a brutal wrestling match going on within every believer. Will the Spirit reign in power, exercising His Lordship over every aspect of our mind, will, and emotions, or will the un-renewed mind, the unbridled will, and our broken and wounded emotions continue their reign of terror over the soul, holding us as hostages to the darkness? Will the life of the old un-renewed self quench the life of the spirit within, or will the new man establish his rule and reign over the soul?

Controlled by the Spirit

The critical issue is our submission to the Lordship of the Spirit. "Now the Lord is the Spirit; and where the Spirit of the Lord is, there is liberty" (2 Corinthians 3:17). When the Holy Spirit – joined to our human spirit – is given His rightful place, He exercises His control by bringing the old man into subjection through the power of the cross. But whenever we shrug off the Lordship of the Spirit, we inadvertently allow the old man to rise up and take control. Paul explained it this way: "If we live in the Spirit, let us also walk in the Spirit" (Galatians 5:25). Just because your spirit man is comprehensively immersed in the Holy Spirit does not automatically guarantee that your entire being – mind, will, emotions, and physical body – will be governed by the Spirit. Paul also said, "This I say then: walk in the Spirit, and you shall not fulfill the lust of the flesh" (Galatians 5:16). It is incumbent on every believer whose spirit is immersed in the Holy Spirit to intentionally walk in the Spirit. We walk in the Spirit by standing in the finished work of the cross and reckoning ourselves dead to sin and alive to God. We walk in the Spirit by refusing to give sin dominion in any part of our body or soul.

The Spirit-filled man or woman is the person who fully submits themselves to the rule and reign of the Holy Spirit's Lordship. They allow Him to take full ownership and possession of their entire being so that He has complete freedom to exercise His dominion. This is how Jesus lived on earth. One of my favourite translations of the New Testament is *Wuest's Expanded Translation of the New Testament*. Kenneth Wuest has a tradition of translating the phrase "filled with the Spirit" as "controlled by the Spirit." For example, he translates Ephesians 5:18 as: "Stop being intoxicated with wine ... but be constantly controlled by the Spirit." Similarly, in many other places in the New Testament Wuest follows this pattern. So we read:

- "Then Peter, being controlled by the Holy Spirit, said...." (Acts 4:8)
- "And they were all controlled by the Holy Spirit." (Acts 4:31)
- "Stephen, a man full of faith and controlled by the Holy Spirit." (Acts 6:6)
- "[Barnabas] was a good man and controlled by the Holy Spirit." (Acts 11:24)

There are many more instances in Wuest's Translation that follow this pattern but I have quoted enough examples to make the point. Whilst our spirit is now fully immersed in the Holy Spirit, the question remains whether we will allow the Holy Spirit to fully immerse and possess our entire being. Whenever we submit to the Lordship of the Holy Spirit there is a flow of the glory and the power of Christ from our spirit to every region of the soul, bringing everything into subjection to the Spirit's control. Romans 8:13 is another of Paul's headline verses: "For if you live according to the flesh you will die; but if by the Spirit you put to death the deeds of the body, you will live" (Romans 8:13). The Spirit is the exclusive agent who implements the power of the cross in our hearts by putting to death all of the works of the flesh. But we have a vital part to play that God cannot and will not do for us. We volitionally choose to *put to death* all that constitutes our old life. But we do this in the power of the Holy Spirit.

Paul said, "Put on the Lord Jesus Christ, and make no provision for the flesh, to fulfill its lusts" (Romans 13:14). There is a continual putting on of Christ and a putting off, or putting to death, everything that constitutes the old self. Every moment we must choose to put on the new man in Christ and put off the old man. We are called to engage, activate, and live out of our spirit man. Jesus instructed His disciples to take up their cross and deny themselves daily, just as He denied Himself daily in order to live and walk perpetually in the Spirit. John Wesley asked the question: "Who will you deny? Yourself or the Lord?" Commenting on Jesus' call to "take up our cross daily" (Luke 9:23), Wesley said:

> Denying ourselves and taking up our cross isn't a little side issue – it is absolutely necessary to becoming or continuing to be a disciple of Jesus. If we don't practice self-denial, we aren't His disciples. It's useless to try to follow the One who was crucified without taking up our own cross daily. Unless we deny ourselves, it will be impossible not to deny the Lord.[15]

Rivers of Living Water

When we choose submission to the Lordship of Christ it releases a flow of the river of God. Rivers of living water flowed out of Jesus when He was on earth. Even in heaven these rivers continually gush forth from the Lamb of God. "And he showed me a pure river of water of life, clear as crystal, proceeding from the throne of God and of the Lamb" (Revelation 22:1). Jesus is the perpetual source of living water.

He said, "It is done! I am the Alpha and the Omega, the Beginning and the End. I will give of the fountain of the water of life freely to him who thirsts" (Revelation 21:6). Because Christ now lives in us, He promised us that these same rivers of living water will flow out of us. "If anyone is thirsty, let him come to Me and drink. He who believes in Me, as the Scripture said, "From his innermost being will flow rivers of living water" (John 7:37-38). You are now a custodian of the river!

This glorious living water flows out of the presence of Christ who already immerses and overflows our human spirit. "Whoever drinks of the water that I shall give him will never thirst. But the water that I shall give him will become in him a fountain of water springing up into everlasting life" (John 4:14). Faith and obedience releases the flow of the river of God. Faith in the finished work of Christ activates the outflow of the rivers of divine love, glory, peace, life, and joy so that these realities overtake and control every part of our lives. In this way, our mind, will, and emotions become a vehicle of expression for the mind of Christ, the will of God, and the emotional wholeness of Jesus.

Faith in Christ opens the floodgate of heaven's supply, releasing the flow of the life of Christ out of the human spirit to touch every region of the soul. "The Lord will guide you continually and satisfy your soul in drought and strengthen your bones; you shall be like a watered garden and like a fountain of water, whose waters do not fail" (Isaiah 58:11). If we truly believe in the finished work of Christ, we will reckon ourselves dead to sin and alive to God, and our faith will activate and open the floodgates of heaven. The church is the New Jerusalem and the Lord promised in the Old Testament that "in that day it shall be that living waters shall flow from Jerusalem..." (Zechariah 14:8). "A fountain shall flow from the temple of the Lord and water the Valley of Acacias" (Joel 3:18). Ezekiel saw a vision of living water flowing out of a mystical temple, which was clearly a prophetic picture of the church.

> Then He brought me back to the door of the temple; and there was water, flowing from under the threshold of the temple toward the east, for the front of the temple faced east; the water was flowing from under the right side of the temple, south of the altar. Everything that touches the water of this river will live. Wherever this water flows, everything will live! (Ezekiel 47:1, 9)

The river never stops flowing out of Jesus! As we stand in faith, there is a flow of living water from our spirit to our soul. Notice the direction of the flow! This river gives life to every part of our soul that was once under the dominion of sin and death! We only need to learn how to open the floodgates and let the river of living water flow out of our innermost being (our spirit) into our soul. Your spirit is continually Spirit-filled to the point of overflowing but, sadly, some Christians never seem to find the lever to activate the floodgates! King David declared prophetically, "There is a river whose streams shall make glad the city of God" (Psalms 46:4). This river satisfies and restores our souls and it fills us with an unimaginable gladness and joy. "They are abundantly satisfied with the fullness of Your house and You give them drink from the river of Your pleasures" (Psalms 36:8).

The Wine of the Spirit

In the Scriptures, another metaphor of the Spirit is that of wine. There is a wild drunken party going on inside your spirit! There is music and dancing in the Father's house. There is so much of the wine of the Spirit flowing inside of you that you could make a thousand people drunk on the love of Christ. David discovered this river of divine love and proclaimed that anyone who discovers this river will be "abundantly satisfied." The Hebrew word he used for this state of deep satisfaction was *ravah,* and it literally means to be "made drunk." The ancient Vulgate Translation said, "They shall be inebriated with the plenty of Thy house and Thou shalt make them drink from the torrent of Thy pleasure" (Psalm 36:8).

David's most famous Psalm contains this phrase: "You prepare a table before me in the presence of my enemies; You anoint my head with oil; My cup runs over" (Psalm 23:5). Again, the most popular translations fail to capture the true meaning of this text, perhaps through fear of promoting drunkenness at the communion table. The term "runs over" in Hebrew is *ravayah* [from the root word *ravah*], and it also means to be inebriated by wine. The Vulgate Translation says, "My chalice which inebriateth me, how goodly is it!"

Paul said, "We were all made to drink of one Spirit" (1 Corinthians 12:13 NASB). You were made to drink. God wants to teach you to be a heavy drinker of the wine of His glory that heals rather than destroys. We are forbidden to get drunk on earthly wine but we are strongly encouraged to get fully inebriated on the wine of the glory of Christ. In Christ there is no such thing as excess. David apparently passed on the secret of this river of heavenly wine to his son, Solomon, who went as far as describing the house of the Lord as the "house of wine." "He has brought me to his banquet hall and his banner over me is love" (Song of Songs 2:4). The "banqueting hall" in Hebrew is *yayin bayith. Yayin* is Hebrew for wine and *bayith* means house. Once again the translators were reluctant to accurately translate the text in order to avoid a potential scandal.

But Solomon takes the revelation a step further in Song of Songs when he actually promotes drunkenness on the glory wine of heaven. The Bridegroom says, "I have drunk my wine and my milk. Eat, O friends, and drink; drink your fill, O lovers" (Song of Songs 5:1). "Drink your fill" in Hebrew is *shakar* and it means to be made completely drunk. The ancient Septuagint Version translated this verse as "Eat, friends, and drink: and be drunk [*shakar*] brothers and sisters!" This is a command to get fully loaded on the wine of heaven.

Do you remember the outpouring of the Spirit in Acts 2 that gave birth to the church? And do you remember the response of the crowd? "Amazed and perplexed, they asked one another, 'What does this mean?' Some, however, made fun of them and said, 'They have had too much wine!'" (Acts 2:12-13 NIV). The church was born in the house of wine, and Holy Spirit drunkenness has characterised many of the great outpourings throughout church history as God's people were overcome with the joy-filled wine of heavenly bliss and intoxication. This wine can lead to ecstatic prophetic encounters that cause the drinker to be lifted out of his mind. Cyril, Bishop of Jerusalem (348 AD), commented on the response of the crowd to the first great outpouring of the wine of Christ's love.

> They are not drunk in the way you might think! But according to that which is written, "They shall be drunken with the fatness of Your house; and You shall make them drink of the torrents of Thy pleasure" (Psalm 36:8). They are indeed drunk, but with the sober intoxication which kills sin and gives life to the heart and which is the opposite of physical drunkenness. Drunkenness makes a person forget what he knows; this kind, instead, brings understanding of things that were not formerly known. They are drunk insofar as they have drunk the wine of that mystical Vine which affirms, "I

139

am the Vine; you are the branches" (John 15:5). For truly, the wine was new, even the grace of the New Testament; but this new wine was from a spiritual Vine.[16]

Saint Ambrose must have also been a secret drinker. He said:

> Every time you drink, you receive the remission of sins and you become intoxicated with the Spirit. It is in that sense that the Apostle said, "Do not get drunk with wine ... but be filled with the Spirit" (Ephesians 5:18). He who becomes intoxicated with wine staggers, but he who becomes intoxicated with the Holy Spirit is rooted in Christ. How truly excellent is this intoxication which produces the sobriety of the soul.[17]

Saint Augustine similarly confessed to more than the occasional sip of the Spirit:

> The Holy Spirit has come to abide in you; do not make Him withdraw; do not exclude Him from your heart in any way. He is a good guest; He found you empty and He filled you; He found you hungry and He satisfied you; He found you thirsty and He has intoxicated you. May He truly intoxicate you! The Apostle said, "Do not be drunk with wine which leads to debauchery." Then, as if to clarify what we should be intoxicated with, he adds, "But be filled with the Spirit, addressing one another in psalms and hymns and spiritual songs, singing and making melody to the Lord with all your heart" (Ephesians 5:18). Does not a person who rejoices in the Lord and sings to Him exuberantly seem like a person who is drunk? I like this kind of intoxication. The Spirit of God is both drink and light![18]

Raniero Cantalamessa, papal preacher to Pope John Paul II's pontifical household, writes:

Saint Augustine asked himself why Scripture had used such a daring image as intoxication. He concluded that it is because only the state of a man who has drunk so much as to lose his mind can give us an idea — even though it is a negative one — of what happens to the human mind when it receives the ineffable joy of the Holy Spirit. The mind recedes and becomes divine, being intoxicated with the abundance in the house of God. When spiritually intoxicated, a person is out of his mind, not because he is bereft of reason, as is the case with wine or drugs, but because he passes beyond reason into the light of God.[19]

Shining Like Stars in the Universe

The flow of the wine of heaven that both inebriates and restores the mind is in many ways like the flow of light that issues forth from the Lamb of God. As Saint Augustine said, "The Spirit of God is both drink and light." Both water and light flow in streams. Just as the river proceeds out of the Lamb, so we find in the book of Revelation that a glorious light also proceeds forth from the Lamb. "The city had no need of the sun or of the moon to shine in it, for the glory of God illuminated it. The Lamb is its light" (Revelation 21:23). Christ proclaimed that He is the "Light of the World" but later told His disciples that they were the light of the world, encouraging them to let their light so shine that men would see their good works and glorify their Father in heaven (Matthew 5:14-16). Because Christ is in us, we actually become light! Paul said, "For you were once darkness, but now *you are light* in the Lord. Walk as children of light" (Ephesians 5:8).

Remember our analogy in chapter two between the human spirit and a star? Before we were born again our dead spirit was like a deep black hole in space. The human spirit without Christ is like a dead star. No light is emitted from a black hole. A black hole absorbs everything. It sucks everything into itself. A black hole is a collapsed star that has imploded and has created a gravitational vortex that now pulls everything into it. Without Christ the depth of our neediness was unfathomable and our thirst was unquenchable. Like a black hole, we drew on everyone around us to fill our need for love and approval. Our massive affirmation deficit made us dependent upon others to meet our need for just a taste of affirming words of acceptance. A black hole is the ultimate picture of the dead human spirit that is so thoroughly self-centred that it seeks to pull everything and everyone into its selfish personal agenda of self-gratification.

Jude called selfish people "wandering stars." "They are shameless in the way they care only about themselves. They are wandering stars, heading for everlasting gloom and darkness" (Jude 12-13 NLT). The Message says they are "lost stars in outer space on their way to the black hole" (Jude 13). Not only are the lost heading for a black hole, they are by nature black holes. Yet God delights in taking spiritual black holes and turning them into radiant stars! As our spirit man is activated through faith in the finished work of Christ, we begin to shine the light of the glory of God. Our faith is in the finished work of Christ for us through death on the cross and the miracle of spiritual rebirth. "It is finished!"

As we stand in the reality of Romans 6, considering ourselves dead to sin and alive to God, we switch on the light and begin to shine forth the glory of the Lord out of our innermost being. Isaiah instructs us to "Arise, shine; for your light has come! And the glory of the Lord is risen upon you" (Isaiah 60:1). The next verse contrasts the two extremes of the darkness of billions of black holes with the brightness of the saints who shine like stars as they radiate the glorious light of God. "Darkness as black as night will cover all the nations of the earth, but the glory of the Lord will shine over you" (Isaiah 60:2 NLT).

I really love the way Paul described true believers as bright and shining stars. "You shine like stars in the universe as you hold out the word of life" (Philippians 2:15-16 NIV). Paul taught that different believers shine with different degrees of luminosity, depending upon their faith in the finished work of Christ and their degree of personal spiritual breakthrough. There are believers who are overcomers and there are believers who are still overcome. "There are also celestial bodies and terrestrial bodies; but the glory of the celestial is one, and the glory of the terrestrial is another. There is one glory of the sun, another glory of the moon, and another glory of the stars; for one star differs from another star in glory. So also is the resurrection of the dead" (1 Corinthians 15:40-42).

In the book of Daniel we read: "Those who are wise will shine like the brightness of the heavens, and those who lead many to righteousness, like the stars for ever and ever" (Daniel 12:3 NIV). John the Baptist was described by Jesus as a "burning and shining light, and you were willing for a time to rejoice in his light" (John 5:35). John was a burning light, but Jesus went on to describe the entire company of His disciples as the light of the world. We can hide that light under a lampstand or we can arise and let it shine. "Assuredly, I say to you, among those born of women there has not risen one greater than John the Baptist; but he who is least in the kingdom of heaven is greater than he" (Matthew 11:11).

Spirit Activated Death

If Christ really is in us as the Scriptures declare, every single Christian has the potential to learn how to activate the flow of love, light, glory, and power from within. "We have this treasure in earthen vessels that the excellence of the power may be of God and not of us" (2 Corinthians 4:7). We are sons and daughters of the resurrection power of God and we switch on these supernatural realities through our faith in the finished work. We have already been baptized into the death and resurrection of Christ. We need a clear vision of the miracle God has performed in our spirit by placing us "in Christ" and establishing us in the reality that we have been both co-crucified and co-resurrected with Christ. We have not just been crucified with Him; we have also been raised up from the spiritual grave with Christ!

> Do you not know that as many of us as were baptized into Christ Jesus were baptized into His death? Therefore we were buried with Him through baptism into death, that just as Christ was raised from the dead by the glory of the Father, even so we also should walk in newness of life. For if we have been united together in the likeness of His death, certainly we also shall be in the likeness of His resurrection. (Romans 6:3-5)

God's solution for the "old man" is the power of the cross. God has already put the old man to death so Paul could truthfully say, "I have been crucified with Christ; it is no longer I who lives, but Christ lives in me" (Galatians 2:20). The old "I" is dead and the Holy Spirit supernaturally and experientially enforces this death as we believe ourselves to be dead to sin and alive to God. Paul taught that the actual mortification of the old man was a work of the Holy Spirit: "But if by the Spirit you are putting to death the deeds of the body, you will live" (Romans 8:13 NASB). We cannot do this in our own strength, but we can do it in the power of the Holy Spirit.

Paul's prayer was: "That I may know Him and the power of His resurrection and the fellowship of His sufferings; being conformed to His death" (Philippians 3:10). The Greek word Paul used for "conformed" was *summorphos,* and it means "jointly formed or united in the same form." It speaks of the supernatural implementation of the fullness of Christ's death to sin through the power of the Holy Spirit. We need a vision for a supernaturally empowered death to sin that is activated through our faith in the finished work of the cross. This is God's answer to sin and the old selfish nature: a supernaturally activated death! We come into agreement with Scripture through faith and the Spirit delivers us from the power of sin and death. This is not self-mortification; this is Spirit mortification.

Opening the Floodgates

God wants to teach us how to open the floodgates and release the torrents of the river of life so that the fullness of life that is in our spirit overflows into our broken souls. We do this by embracing the cross of Christ. We are the immediate beneficiaries of the rivers of living water that flow out of our innermost being. It flows through our lives to bless others but we cannot give away what we haven't received. So we must learn how to open the floodgates of this river of love, joy, and peace.

There is a river of love that God wants to release from our spirit into our souls. This love has the power to wash away all bitterness and resentment and bring healing to all of our emotional brokenness. John, the mystic Apostle, intoxicated by this river of love, cried out, "Behold what manner of love the Father has lavished upon us" (1 John 3:1). God intends to open the floodgates of His unconditional love like a torrential waterfall out of your innermost spirit. "Deep calls to deep in the roar of Your waterfalls; all Your waves and breakers have swept over me" (Psalm 42:7).

David said, "You give them drink from your river of delights" (Psalm 36:8 NIV). The Vulgate Translation says, "You shall make them drink from the torrent of Your pleasure." This word "torrent" prophesies a mighty rushing waterfall that is powerful enough to knock us off our feet and sweep us away in the torrential flood of divine love. "The floods have lifted up their voice, the floods lift up their pounding waves. More than the sounds of many waters, than the mighty breakers of the sea, the Lord on high is mighty" (Psalm 93:3-4 NASB).

Do you believe there is a torrential river of love that can flood and overwhelm your soul? The Scriptures reveal that this river is locked up inside of you, awaiting activation through faith in the revelation of Christ in you, the hope of glory. The Bridegroom says to His bride, "You are a garden locked up, my sister, my bride; you are a spring enclosed, a sealed fountain" (Song of Songs 4:12 NIV). But the Bridegroom wants to unlock and open the sealed fountain so the living waters of His great love begin to flow out of our spirit to nourish the garden of our soul.

Just as there is a mighty river of love, there is also a river of joy that has the power to overwhelm and restore our souls. "There is a river whose streams shall make glad the city of God" (Psalm 46:4). "Gladness" in Hebrew [*sameach*] means "to make joyful, to brighten up." The NLT says, "A river brings joy to the city of our God." God has promised that this river will actually overtake, or overwhelm, the saints. "The ransomed of the Lord will return. They will enter Zion with singing; everlasting joy will crown their heads. Gladness and joy *will overtake them*, and sorrow and sighing will flee away" (Isaiah 51:11 NIV).

In the same way, there is peace like a river that supernaturally delivers the soul from all torment and fear. "For thus says the Lord: "Behold, I will extend peace to her like a river" (Isaiah 66:12). "'Peace and prosperity will overflow Jerusalem like a river,' says the Lord" (Isaiah 66:12 NLT). "The Lord will comfort Israel again and make her deserts blossom. Her barren wilderness will become as beautiful as Eden – the garden of the Lord. Joy and gladness will be found there. Lovely songs of thanksgiving will fill the air" (Isaiah 51:3 NLT). Love, joy, and peace are the primary fruits of the Spirit that overflow our souls and transform our interior life into a glorious garden. If our soul feels like a barren wasteland, when God has promised to turn it into a

Garden of Eden, we need to ask ourselves if we are activating the flow of the river into our souls.

This river of love, joy, and peace that flows out of our innermost being converges into a torrent of bliss and ecstasy. Part of Jesus' ministry in our lives is the ministry of heavenly bliss. "Christ arrived as the High Priest of the bliss that was to be..." (Hebrews 9:11 Moffatt Translation). What is bliss? Bliss is a state of extreme happiness; it is the joy of heaven and the ecstasy of supernatural encounter. Bliss is the experiential convergence of the supernatural love, joy, and peace of Christ. It is like a divine cocktail of blessedness mixed by our Great High Priest who delights in intoxicating us and overtaking our souls with the wine of ecstasy. The word "bliss" is a cognate of the English word "bless."

The most important thing is to recognise the direction of the flow. The born again experience is described as a conversion. When God regenerated the human spirit, He reversed its polarity! Instead of our spirit functioning as a massive gravitational vortex, the polarity has been completely reversed and now the automatic flow of the current is outward from our spirit man. God wants to impart a powerful revelatory vision of the rivers of living water and the radiant light of Christ flowing out of our innermost being. He wants to flood our souls and, ultimately, to flow through our lives to meet the needs of others. But we cannot give away what we haven't yet experientially received. The greater our vision of the glorious new creation, the more we will be able to access the unlimited reservoir of divine blessings. We will be able to activate the flow for our own restoration and the restoration of others.

The river of bliss can become so intense that it throws believers into a state of pure heavenly ecstasy. The New Testament uses the word Greek word *ekstasis* seven times. This word is transliterated into the English word "ecstasy" and it describes a state in which someone is thrown or lifted out of their mind with such intense emotion that it transports them into another place. The translators of the New Testament most commonly used the word "trance" to describe this state where the subject was entranced by the intensity of the glory realm of heaven. *Ekstasis* is derived from *existemi,* which means to be thrust into a state of astonishment so as to be beside one's self with amazement. *Existemi* appears eighteen times in the New Testament, always referring to the result of intense supernatural activity.

Ecstasy is a peak spiritual experience induced through a supernatural encounter with the glory of God. In these experiences believers are seized or "lifted outside of themselves" into such an intense absorption in the glory of God that it interrupts their ordinary consciousness of space and time. Hence, the somewhat intimidating word: *trance.* The important thing to note concerning this peak experience is that this intense spiritual reality also flows out of the indwelling of the Holy Spirit in our heart. Ecstasy can seize a believer with such physical force that the believer can shake violently or spin. True divine ecstasy also thrusts the believer into an intense prophetic encounter with God, where heavenly realities become overwhelmingly real and powerful.

"Bless the Lord, O my soul and forget not all His benefits" (Psalm 103:2). God doesn't want us to forget His benefits so He continually reveals them to, and confers them upon, our hearts. "Blessed be the Lord who daily loads us with benefits" (Psalms 68:19). All of these benefits of supernatural love, joy, peace, bliss, and ecstasy flow out of the fullness of the Holy Spirit who is joined to our spirit. Activating these powerful new creation realities will confer tremendous spiritual benefits upon us personally, but also upon those people who come into contact with us. The more we comprehend by revelation the reality of Who lives inside of us, the more we will be likely to see these strong manifestations of the Spirit become evident in our personal lives. This is the destiny of all those who have been fully immersed into the Spirit of Christ.

Chapter Eleven

An Entirely New Core Identity

The miracle that God has performed inside of our hearts by the washing and renewing of our spirit, giving us a brand new heart, and bestowing the free gift of righteousness upon us has extraordinary implications for our core identity. The work of the Holy Spirit in the miracle of the new creation has resulted in us receiving a brand new identity that has been supernaturally bestowed upon us by God.

The self-help movement vainly tries to reshape a person's self image through positive thinking and positive self affirmation. But no amount of thinking positively about ourselves or attempts to construct a healthy self image will ever substitute for what God has already done in the heart of the believer. If we are truly new creations in Christ, there is an imperative to discover what God has already done or we will spend all our energy trying in our own strength to do something that God has already done. Identity comes from the Lord!

Core identity is one of the greatest issues facing human beings today. "Who am I?" is the cry of every heart. People desperately want to know who they are. We are so desperate to find an answer to this question that we even go as far as "test driving" personalities in order to try to create a sense of identity and significance that will result in our acceptance by others. If there is anything that is still striving to prove ourselves to others, that is an indicator that we still need an upgrade in our core identity.

Identity confusion comes in all forms. Every human being suffers from identity confusion to one degree or another but sometimes this identity confusion can become acute. The contemporary phenomenon of *Gender Identity Confusion* is ultimately a symptom of people's alienation from God. The transgender community exists because some people are not bonded or reconciled to their own gender. There are men who actually believe they are women and there are women who actually believe they are men. Transvestitism, or cross dressing, is an early indicator of gender confusion. Some people who struggle with this issue undergo a full surgical sex change as the result of a long journey of gender confusion.

Gender confusion usually develops very early because our sexuality is a major part of our core identity. If people do not bond in early life with their own gender, then major developmental disorders will surely follow. Transgender behaviour would be entirely acceptable were it not for the existence of God. God relates to every human being as either male or female. He calls us either son or daughter. Jesus said, "Have you not read that He who made them at the beginning *'made them male and female'*" (Matthew 19:4). It is God who bestows a sense of true sexual identity upon a human being. Christians who undergo the full sex change claim passionately that God has told them they are females in a male body or males in a female body. For them true freedom only comes through surgery. But this would imply that God has made a mistake in creation.

From a biblical perspective we can confidently say that God bestows a masculine gender upon those with a male physical body and a female gender upon those in a female body. God relates to every human being either as a man or as a woman, just as a mother and father relate to their children as either male or female on the basis of their physical bodies. Gender confusion is an excellent example of the identity crisis in our contemporary culture. All of us have a core identity bestowed by God whether we intentionally embrace it or not. Not only has God initially created us either male or female, He has recreated us as new creations with a brand new core identity of either sonship or daughter-ship. "For we are His workmanship, **created** in Christ Jesus" (Ephesians 2:10).

The Orphan Spirit

For all human beings their **default** core identity is that of an "orphan." An orphan has no deep sense of family or belonging: they feel very much alone! Orphans struggle continually with rejection and abandonment. From God's perspective, the world is a giant orphanage in which billions of orphans are desperately trying to discover or create a sense of personal identity. All parents seek to bestow a sense of family identity upon their children but that is never enough to touch the core of our being. Even people from good Christian homes can, and do, suffer from this sense of being orphaned. The so-called "orphan spirit" is the product of our alienation from God. Paul said, "Once you were alienated from God" (Colossians 1:21 NIV). No amount of excellent parenting can produce freedom from this core identity crisis. The deepest freedom from our the orphan identity only comes from God.

Interestingly, Jesus regarded **everyone** as orphans. He identified both the condition and the solution. He said, "I will not leave you as orphans; I will come to you" (John 14:18 NIV). His promise to come to us in our orphan identity crisis and to reconcile us to His Father is the only solution to this universal human dilemma. Only God can bestow a sense of true core identity upon someone. This means that, apart from the establishment of an intimate relationship with God, we will inevitably struggle with our core identity. For some this may lead to gender identity confusion, but for others it may lead to a deep sense of abandonment, fear, or a sense of being completely alone.

It is common in charismatic church circles to hear people use the term "orphan spirit." Usually this can be understood to mean an orphan identity. But there is a deep truth hidden in the term orphan spirit, because the human spirit defiled by sin and dead to God is orphaned in the full sense of the term. In chapter twelve we will explore the concept of God as the "Father of spirits" (Hebrews 12:9). When God gives us a brand new spirit, He rips the old orphan identity right out of our heart and bestows a perfect new core identity of sonship upon us through one miraculous creative act. Therefore, the key to experientially overcoming the old orphan identity is to receive deep revelation into who we now are in Christ, the beloved Son.

The Story of Carlina White

In January 2011, I was on holiday with my wife in New Zealand, sitting in a cafe reading the paper, when my eyes fell upon a remarkable story. It was the story of a American woman named Carlina White who had been kidnapped as a nineteen-day-old baby from a New York hospital. Her kidnapper was a woman who was childless. This woman became so desperate to have her own daughter that she masqueraded as a nurse and stole Carlina, who was sick in hospital. The true mother and father of the child were understandably devastated by their loss. Throughout the painful years and decades that followed, they always sensed that their baby girl was alive and out there in the world somewhere. Little did they know that she was raised about seventy kilometres (forty-three miles) away, under a false identity.

This false identity and false name was imposed upon little Carlina by the woman who raised her as her pretend mother. But something didn't add up for young Carlina. As she grew up she sensed she

152

was too different from her "family" to be the child of her kidnapper. When she was sixteen she asked her mother for her birth certificate to get her driver's licence, but the mother couldn't produce one. This contributed to Carlina's gnawing suspicion that something was desperately wrong. When she was twenty-three years old, the conviction that she was not a legitimate part of her so-called family reached fever pitch. The newspaper reported:

> Three days before Christmas a young woman in Atlanta called the National Center for Missing and Exploited Children and said, "I don't know who I am." She has now been given an answer: she was not Nejdra Nance of Connecticut. Her real name was Carlina White, born in Harlem and snatched as a baby from a hospital in a case that stunned the city.

She was eventually re-united with her true family and one of America's most extraordinary cases of a missing person was finally solved. The newspaper story continued:

> "It's like being born again," she said. "I feel like I'm in a dream. I see my face in both my parents." She flew in again on Wednesday night for a second reunion, bringing her young daughter, to start reconstructing her life. "When I see my mother I see myself. I see the smile, the lips, the chin," she told The New York Post. "They were always there, but just missing. Now I feel complete!"

As I read this compelling and moving story one line out of the newspaper report jumped out at me. "In her teens she began to have doubts about her identity." I was so struck by this story and, in particular, this one comment concerning identity that I knew immediately God was speaking to me about this issue of our spiritual identity as sons and daughters of God. Carlina felt like an orphan and the woman who kidnapped her tried desperately to impose an entirely new false identity upon her. But Carlina knew intuitively that this was not her true identity, and she did not rest until she discovered who she really was. The kidnapper is a picture of the devil, who is an identity thief. He comes to rob us of our true identity by continually lying to us, telling us that our true Father doesn't even exist. But Carlina's life story is a wonderful picture of the quest for a sense of homecoming and belonging that will never be satisfied with lies.

We initially come to the Father as orphans, but the Father is at work within our hearts to deliver every one of His sons and daughters from this old orphan identity. But sometimes, even those in the church behave like orphans when they strive to carve out their own sense of identity independently of the Father. There is still so much posturing and performing amongst the saints. The consequence of this unsatisfied longing is that some churches seem more like giant orphanages instead of places that exude a sense of security and belonging. We are sons and daughters who don't really know who we are. We strive for acceptance, working hard to cultivate a sense of personal identity. We perform in order to win the acceptance of our peers, often never understanding that all of our striving is a manifestation of living out of the old orphan identity.

This is all a part of the warfare of the saints as we learn how to deal with the endless barrage of lies concerning our true identity. Satan's primary assignment is to rob us of our true identity. "The thief comes only to steal and kill and destroy; I have come that they may have life, and have it to the full" (John 10:10). Satan is an identity thief. He is also an experienced liar. "When he lies, he speaks his native language, for he is a liar and the father of lies" (John 8:44 NIV). Day and night the devil assaults us with a barrage of identity lies. Just like Carlina's kidnapper, the devil continually bestows a false identity upon us. But eventually, like Carlina, we begin to have doubts about our true identity. We need to come to terms with the fact that the devil continually seeks to impose an orphan identity upon us. He relentlessly lies to us about the nature of God and he desperately hopes we will believe his lie that for some reason, we are not acceptable to our Father.

The Spirit of Adoption

God's solution to the orphan spirit is the Spirit of adoption. Paul expounds on this during his brilliant treatise on the power of the new creation. "For you did not receive the spirit of bondage again to fear, but you received *the Spirit of adoption* by whom we cry out, 'Abba, Father'" (Romans 8:15). The NIV calls this the "Spirit of Sonship."

> For you did not receive a spirit that makes you a slave again to fear, but you received the Spirit of sonship. And by Him we cry, "Abba, Father." The Spirit himself testifies with our spirit that we are God's children. Now if we are children, then we are heirs – heirs of God and co-heirs with Christ. (Romans 8:15-17 NIV)

Let's look at this passage in the New Living Translation:

> You should not be like cowering, fearful slaves. You should behave instead like God's very own children, *adopted* into his family – calling him "Father, dear Father." For his Holy Spirit speaks to us deep in our hearts and tells us that we are God's children. And since we are His children, we will share His treasures – for everything God gives to His Son, Christ, is ours, too!

The Holy Spirit continually testifies to our human spirit that we are now sons and daughters in the full sense of the term. Paul clearly loved the redemptive power of this theme of adoption. He discussed it in both the book of Romans and in the book of Galatians. Indeed, the reality of our adoption – the singular biblical truth that most powerfully demolishes every lie concerning the orphan spirit – is the centrepiece of Paul's theology of what it means to be a new creation.

But when the fullness of the time had come, God sent forth His Son, born of a woman, born under the law, to redeem those who were under the law, that we might receive *the adoption as sons*. And because you are sons, God has sent forth the Spirit of His Son into your hearts, crying out, "Abba, Father!" Therefore you are no longer a slave but a son, and if a son, then an heir of God through Christ." (Galatians 4:4-7)

The Father has had an eternal plan to adopt us as sons and daughters and to establish us in this revelatory truth to such an extent that it deals a decisive death blow to our old orphan identity.

Long ago, even before He made the world, God loved us and chose us in Christ to be holy and without fault in His eyes. His unchanging plan has always been to *adopt us* into His own family by bringing us to Himself through Jesus Christ. And this gave Him great pleasure. So we praise God for the wonderful kindness He has poured out on us because *we belong* to His dearly loved Son." (Ephesians 1:4-6 NLT)

We belong! God is continually lavishing *a sense of belonging* upon us. We are accepted in the Beloved Son. "To the praise of the glory of His grace, by which He has made us accepted in the Beloved" (Ephesians 1:6). The Father continually spoke unconditional acceptance over His Beloved Son. "And suddenly a voice came from heaven, saying, 'This is My beloved Son, in whom I am well pleased'" (Matthew 3:17). To be unconditionally accepted in the Beloved Son means that we are accepted by the Father just as Jesus is accepted by the Father. The impartation of the "Spirit of sonship" means that we have equal status with the Son of God before our Father in Heaven. The Father sees us as being "**IN** the Beloved Son" or "**IN** Christ." In this way, Jesus' core identity of sonship is comprehensively and fully transferred to us.

Core Acceptance and Identity

God continues to prophetically speak acceptance and adoption over us until we believe it in the core of our being. Believing it intellectually is not enough. It only comes through **encounter** as a profound mystical experience. We call these revelatory love encounters "Father encounters," and they are the key to identity transformation. The fruit of these revelatory encounters are a deep sense of belonging and security. Our Father says, "Whoever listens to Me will dwell safely and will be **secure**, without fear of evil" (Proverbs 1:33). "My people will dwell in a peaceful habitation; in secure dwellings, and in quiet resting places" (Isaiah 32:18). A secure person doesn't have to strive to impress others. These kinds of revelatory love encounters decisively demolish all performance based approval in the hearts of God's children. Through these kinds of supernatural experiences we learn how to become a "human being" rather than a "human doing."

Royal Sons and Daughters

A series of significant spiritual transitions await every believer who is growing in the Spirit. First God transitions us from orphans to sons and then from sons to royal kings. God bestows a deep sense of royalty upon His sons and daughters. We cannot attain our royal identity without being established in sonship first. These are the prophetic declarations that God makes over His sons and daughters: "You are a chosen generation, a **royal priesthood**, a holy nation" (1 Peter 2:9). He is the King and as sons and daughters we have also become royalty. The royalty of King Jesus is bestowed upon us. "In that day the Lord of hosts will become a beautiful crown and a glorious diadem to the remnant of His people" (Isaiah 28:5 NASB). Jesus bestows His own royal identity upon His brethren.

God gives us an entirely new name, which speaks of our new identity. "The nations will see your righteousness and all kings your glory; and you will be called by *a new name* which the mouth of the Lord will designate. You will also be a crown of beauty in the hand of the Lord and *a royal diadem* in the hand of your God" (Isaiah 62:2-3 NASB). If you are born from above you now live in the palace of the King. Everything He has is yours. Immediately after Paul taught about the Spirit of sonship in Romans 8, he began teaching about inheritance. "And since we are His children, we will share His treasures – for everything God gives to His Son, Christ, is ours, too (Romans 8:17 NLT).

After God has delivered us from our old orphan identity, He seeks to transition us into a place where we begin to sense our true royalty. It is necessary for prophets to "explain to the people the behaviour of royalty" (1 Samuel 10:25). Receiving this sense of royalty is a prerequisite to us entering into our full inheritance as sons and daughters. Our inheritance is so outrageously royal and lavish that we cannot step into it if we are still bound by old mindsets and an old identity.

The Story of Mephibosheth

There is an incredible story in the Old Testament about a young man who had a low self image because he was orphaned by his deceased father. Nevertheless, this young man was able to transition into a new royal identity. His name was Mephibosheth. I absolutely love this story because it speaks so powerfully to me about the amazing transformation God has wrought within my own heart on my personal journey from orphan to son to heir.

> Jonathan, son of Saul, had a son who was lame in both feet. He was five years old when the news about Saul and Jonathan came from Jezreel. His nurse picked him up and fled, but as she hurried to leave, he fell and became crippled. His name was Mephibosheth. (2 Samuel 4:4 NIV)

When David became King he remembered his covenant with Jonathan. David asked, "Is there anyone still left of the house of Saul to whom I can show kindness for Jonathan's sake?" Now there was a servant of Saul's household named Ziba. They called him to appear before David, and the king said to him, "Are you Ziba?" "Your servant," he replied. The king asked, "Is there no one still left of the house of Saul to whom I can show God's kindness?" Ziba answered the king, "There is still a son of Jonathan; he is crippled in both feet." "Where is he?" the king asked. Ziba answered, "He is in Lo Debar." So King David had him brought from Lo Debar. When Mephibosheth came to David, he bowed down to pay him honour. David said, "Mephibosheth?" "Your servant," he replied. "Don't be afraid," David said to him, "for I will surely show you kindness for the sake of your father Jonathan. I will restore to you all the land that belonged to your grandfather Saul, and *you will always eat at my table.*" Mephibosheth bowed down and said, "What is your servant, that you should notice *a dead dog like me?*" Then the king summoned Ziba, Saul's servant, and said to him, "I have given your master's grandson everything that belonged to Saul and his family. You and your sons and your servants are to farm the land for him and bring in the crops, so that your master's grandson may be provided for. And Mephibosheth, grandson of your master, will always eat at my table." Then Ziba said to the king, "Your servant will do whatever my lord the king commands his servant to do." So Mephibosheth ate at David's table like one of the king's sons. (2 Samuel 9:1-11)

Like Mephibosheth, we come into the palace crippled and lame. Our self image is not unlike Mephibosheth's: "*a dead dog like me!*" He felt deeply ashamed because he felt useless because of his injuries. Curiously, "Mephibosheth" means "the one who dispels shame." Jonathan named him as a prophetic decree over his life. But he could only enter into the prophetic destiny of his name if the shame of his own orphan identity was first removed. David treated Mephibosheth as though he was his very own son! King David bestowed the identity of sonship and royalty upon him until he became accustomed to sitting at the king's own table. David also gave him a great inheritance. What an awesome picture of redemption! Dining at the King's table lifts the shame from our lives and establishes us in a new core identity of sonship and royalty.

Jesus longs to host us at His table and to sit and eat with each of us as if we were the only one at His table. We are seated at the King's table on His immediate left. David said, "I have set the Lord always before me; because He is at my right hand I shall not be moved" (Psalm 16:8). Jesus Himself invites His brethren to dine at His royal table.

> Behold, I stand at the door and knock; if anyone hears My voice and opens the door, I will come in to him and ***will dine with him***, and he with Me. He who overcomes, I will grant to him to sit down with Me on My throne, as I also overcame and sat down with My Father on His throne. He who has an ear, let him hear what the Spirit says to the churches. (Revelation 3:20-22 NASB)

The Coronation of King Saul

Transitioning into a sense of authentic royalty doesn't come naturally. There is another story of the first king in the nation of Israel. Israel had never had a king and Saul had his own set of personal issues that significantly hindered him in coming to terms with the royalty that was suddenly thrust upon him. Saul's grandson, Mephibosheth, suffered from a very poor self image and it is probable that this had come down the bloodline from his grandfather.

> When Samuel brought all the tribes of Israel near, the tribe of Benjamin was chosen. Then he brought forward the tribe

of Benjamin, clan by clan, and Matri's clan was chosen. Finally Saul son of Kish was chosen. But when they looked for him, he was not to be found. So they inquired further of the Lord, "Has the man come here yet?" And the Lord said, "Yes, *he has hidden himself among the baggage.*" They ran and brought him out, and as he stood among the people he was a head taller than any of the others. Samuel said to all the people, "Do you see the man the Lord has chosen? There is no one like him among all the people." Then the people shouted, "Long live the king!" Then Samuel explained to the people *the behaviour of royalty*, and wrote it in a book and laid it up before the Lord. And Samuel sent all the people away, every man to his house. (1 Samuel 10:20-25)

We are all royal sons and daughters hiding in the midst of our own spiritual baggage. It is this baggage that hinders us from rising up as royal kings and queens in God's kingdom. Our orphan baggage also blinds us to the ways of royalty. It takes a royal mindset to partake of the fullness of the King's palace. If we think like paupers, we will never enjoy the privileges of royalty. We need to transition from orphans to sons and then from sons to royalty! But all we are doing is getting in touch with the new core identity that God bestowed upon us when we were born into the Kingdom. Our new identity is rooted in the reality of the new creation. Our spirit is comprehensively royal and crowned with glory from the moment of the new birth. But it is only the overcomers who enter into the experience of this new identity of sonship and royalty. Like the mythic story of Peter, Susan, Edmund, and Lucy in *The Lion, the Witch and the Wardrobe*, none of us are accustomed to sitting on a throne.

In the book of Revelation, Jesus gave seven promises to those who overcome. Each promise is true of every born again believer, even though it can only be experienced by those who overcome the enemies of their own soul. Remember the promise we read in Isaiah earlier in this chapter? "You shall be called by *a new name* which the mouth of the Lord will name" (Isaiah 62:2). In the book of Revelation Jesus said, "To him who overcomes I will give some of the hidden manna to eat. And I will give him a white stone, and on the stone *a new name* written which no one knows except him who receives it" (Revelation 2:17). In Roman times, the white stone served as an admission ticket into important public events.

The new name written on the white stone speaks of our new identity. This new identity was bestowed upon us when we were born again. However, it is only as we overcome the false orphan identity that the devil has placed upon us, that we experientially enter into the pure enjoyment of admission into the Father's house as sons and into the royal palace as kings and queens. Jesus also said, "To him who overcomes I will grant to sit with Me on My throne, as I also overcame and sat down with My Father on His throne" (Revelation 3:21). Every born again believer is seated with Christ in heavenly places from the moment of the new birth. But we can only fully enter into this reality experientially as we transition into embracing our royal identity. We are "training for reigning!"

God lavished this new identity on us. He prophetically and relentlessly calls out the treasure inside us until we actually begin to believe what He says. God continually testifies with our human spirit that we are His beloved children. "And since we are his children, we will share His treasures – for everything God gives to His Son, Christ, is ours, too" (Romans 8:17 NLT). These are the treasures of royalty. But we cannot possess our inheritance without having our mind renewed to embrace a royal mindset that delivers us from poverty. The ultimate treasure is a brand new spirit that delivers us from our old orphan spirit. "We have this treasure in earthen vessels" (2 Corinthians 4:7). God speaks to the treasure inside of us and awakens our sense of sonship and royalty to prepare us to receive the ultimate royal inheritance of kings.

Chapter Twelve

Aligning Ourselves with the Cross

In light of the new creation miracle, Paul could boldly and confidently proclaim that "old things have passed away; behold all things are new." But many believers secretly wonder if this verse is really true. So many Christians I have spoken to feel that, in spite of the new birth and the truth of our deep mystical union with Christ, there is still a prevailing sense that the old things continue to persist in our lives. This is the universal struggle of Christians until we begin to learn how to align ourselves with the fact of our co-crucifixion with Christ.

Paul could say, "I have been crucified with Christ" because, by faith, he chose to bring himself into a complete alignment with the fact of his personal, historical co-crucifixion with Christ. The truth of Paul's co-crucifixion was based upon what God had done in Jesus on the cross and on what God had already wrought in his heart through the miracle of the new creation. Our co-crucifixion is a fact but there is a part we must play in activating this powerful new creation reality. We dare not overlook the fact that there is a necessity – a biblical imperative – to come into agreement and alignment with this new creation fact. No one else can do it for you. It is a choice that every believer must make every minute of every day as we exercise our faith in the finished work of Christ.

163

The New Testament confronts us with the fact of who we now are in Christ since the moment we first believed. At the very centre of your being, in your spirit, you are comprehensively new. Your old, unregenerate spirit has indeed passed away, and your spirit man has been made entirely new because of the free gift of righteousness. In the centre of your being you are completely alive to God and dead to sin. This is a biblical fact for everyone who has placed their trust in Jesus for salvation. However, *we spend the rest of our lives becoming who we already are in Christ.* For Paul, the cross was the power of God (1 Corinthians 1:18). If we want to experience the resurrection power of Christ in our personal life we must come into alignment with a powerful new creation truth.

Through our mystical union with Christ we are indeed dead to sin to the same extent that Jesus is dead to sin. We are co-crucified, co-buried, and co-risen with Him. His death to sin on the cross was our death to sin. John said, "Whoever has been born of God does not sin, for His seed remains in him; and he cannot sin, because he has been born of God" (1 John 3:9). Our new nature in Christ is not a sin nature; it is now characterised by righteousness and true holiness. Paul said that the new man has been "created according to God, in true righteousness and holiness" (Ephesians 4:24). We must first come to terms with the truth of our co-crucifixion and co-resurrection with Christ. That is the starting point for all personal spiritual breakthrough in walking as a new creation.

According to Paul, when Jesus died, we died. Paul said, "We judge thus: that if One died for all, then ***all died***" (2 Corinthians 5:14). Hence, Paul could confidently declare to every true believer, "For you died, and your life is now hidden with Christ in God" (Colossians 3:3 NIV). When He was buried in the grave, we were buried with Him in the grave. Paul said, "Therefore we were buried with Him through baptism into death" (Romans 6:4). All of these concepts are presented to those who believe as unwavering certainties and solid facts concerning who we are in Christ. Crucifixion with Christ is not something we achieve, it is something we activate through faith in what God has already done.

Paul also affirms our co-resurrection with Him. "But God, who is rich in mercy, because of His great love with which He loved us, even when we were dead in trespasses, *made us alive together with Christ* (by grace you have been saved), and *raised us up together*, and made us sit together in the heavenly places in Christ Jesus" (Ephesians 2:4-6). We are resurrected ones! When Christ rose from the dead we rose from the dead with Him. These are glorious and powerful truths that unequivocally reveal the actual reality of who we are in Christ as new creations. My human spirit is now just as alive to God as Jesus Himself is alive to God. This is why we can confess 2 Corinthians 5:17 as an absolute fact: "Therefore, if anyone is in Christ, he is a new creation; old things have passed away; behold, all things have become new."

But there is another dimension to Paul's preaching that recognises the process through which we come into an experiential alignment with this new creation reality in our human spirit. For Paul, there was a necessity to come into alignment with what is already true in our spirit man. Every single fibre of our being must be brought into conformity with the new creation. Every thought in our mind, every emotion in our heart, and every choice of our will must be brought into conformity to Christ. Paul taught that we are being conformed to the very image of Christ and that this work of the Spirit is a process that involves our daily choice to align ourselves with the fullness of the work of the cross.

Paul called this process "being conformed to His death." He considered it a present-tense work of the Spirit. In Philippians, Paul said that it was his personal goal to "know Him and the power of His resurrection, and the fellowship of His sufferings, ***being conformed to His death,*** if, by any means, I may attain to the resurrection from the dead. Not that I have already attained, or am already perfected; but I press on, that I may lay hold of that for which Christ Jesus has also laid hold of me" (Philippians 3:10-12). This systematic and progressive conformity to the death of Jesus only occurs in our heart as we say yes to the power of the cross every moment of every day.

Whenever we choose to live for ourselves we deny the reality of who we are as new creations. "If One died for all, then all died; and He died for all, that those who live *should live no longer for themselves*, but for Him who died for them and rose again" (2 Corinthians 5:14-15). Because we have been co-crucified with Christ there is a moment by moment choice to either live for ourselves or to live for Christ. Paul had made that choice; he was going to live out the reality of who he was in Christ as a brand new creation. Those who have died to sin in Him are under obligation to no longer live for themselves. They must choose daily to live through the power of the cross.

The Flesh

Jesus has entered our hearts and declared war on the flesh. But what exactly is the flesh? I once heard a preacher say that in order to understand the "flesh" we should drop the "h" off the end of the word and then spell it backward. That, of course, spells "self" and that is an excellent definition of the flesh. The flesh includes the mind, will, and emotions, as well as the physical body when it is under the rule and reign of our old selfish self. The flesh is our old selfish nature that is entirely oriented around self. It is a self-centred state of existence. Hence, a person who is "in the flesh" is a thoroughly self-centred person. Paul emphatically taught "that those who live should live no longer for themselves, but for Him who died for them and rose again" (2 Corinthians 5:15). That means we are to no longer live for self, to serve our selfish desires and inclinations. Instead, we are now to live for Christ!

I like the way The Message Bible paraphrases parts of the New Testament, especially when it comes to dealing with abstract and obscure theological terms such as "the flesh." This translation, like no other, sheds considerable light upon the essence of the flesh.

> Obsession with *self* in these matters is a dead end; attention to God leads us out into the open, into a spacious, free life. Focusing on the *self* is the opposite of focusing on God. Anyone completely absorbed in self ignores God, [and] ends up thinking more about *self* than God. That person ignores who God is and what He is doing." (Romans 8:6-7)

One of the great virtues of *The Message Bible* is its explanation of the flesh. In that significant passage in Galatians where Paul discusses the war between the flesh and the Spirit, The Message Bible says:

> My counsel is this: Live freely, animated and motivated by God's Spirit. Then you won't feed the compulsions of selfishness. For there is a root of sinful self-interest in us that is at odds with a free Spirit, just as the free Spirit is incompatible with selfishness. These two ways of life are antithetical. (Galatians 5:16-17)

We are all familiar with Paul's exhortation in Galatians chapter six to sow to the Spirit instead of sowing to the flesh. But consider how The Message Bible paraphrases this well known passage.

> Don't be misled: No one makes a fool of God. What a person plants, he will harvest. The person who plants selfishness, ignoring the needs of others—ignoring God—harvests a crop of weeds. All he'll have to show for his life is weeds! But the one who plants in response to God, letting God's Spirit do the growth work in him, harvests a crop of real life, eternal life. (Galatians 6:7-8)

Some people question whether we still have a sinful nature while others assert that it doesn't even exist. Paul says, "For we know that our old self was crucified with him so that the body of sin might be done away with, that we should no longer be slaves to sin" (Romans 6:6 NIV). Let me ask you this question: Has your propensity toward selfishness totally disappeared now that you are a new creation in Christ? If you made selfish choices for decades before turning to Christ, did you suddenly stop making those selfish choices the day you were born again? If our selfishness somehow supernaturally disappeared at the new birth, then Paul's exhortations to "put to death" the deeds of the flesh and to make righteous choices would appear rather facetious. Similarly, the references to the ongoing warfare between the flesh and the Spirit would also be redundant, even potentially deceptive. Paul clearly believed and understood that, even though God has miraculously made us new creations, our propensity to step back into a selfish state of existence is always only one bad choice away.

If we define the flesh as a selfish state of human existence, in contrast to a life in the Spirit, which is a Christ-centred state of existence, it becomes crystal clear that there are simply two ways in which we can now choose to walk. Christians can still potentially "walk in the flesh" by making selfish choices or we can "walk in the Spirit" by crucifying those old selfish ways and choosing to live a life centred upon Christ who now lives in our heart. Why does the Bible continually exhort us to love one another? It does so because our continual temptation to walk in our old selfish ways are antithetical to walking in love.

Before Christ entered our lives we had no options: we were doomed to live a life in the flesh. As new creations in Christ, we may now have the option to walk in love and to find an entirely new way to live our lives with Christ at the centre. However, there is no certainty that we will choose to walk in this way. Praise God that we now have a viable alternative to sin and selfishness. This new option creates a new imperative to train ourselves to live in the power of the new creation.

Once we are born again through the Holy Spirit and we find our-selves in Christ, it is the ministry of the Father, the Son, and the Holy Spirit to search out and reveal the depths of residual sin and selfish-ness. This ministry is meant to promote and release the life and heart of Jesus Christ in us. Paul recognized that there was still a residual car-nality in the church that needed to be purged from each believer ex-perientially. "I could not speak to you as to spiritual people but as to carnal, as to babes in Christ" (1 Corinthians 3:1). Rather than telling the Corinthians that their old fleshly nature no longer existed, Paul systematically worked through the issues to disentangle the believers from everything that had been rendered old because of the advent of the new. Paul could call certain born again believers carnal or fleshly because they were still entangled in sinful behaviours and mindsets. The writer to the Hebrews called this "the sin that so easily entangles" (Hebrews 12:1 NIV).

Jesus addressed the responsibility of every true follower to take up his cross daily. "If anyone desires to come after Me, let him deny himself, and take up his cross daily, and follow Me" (Luke 9:23). Christians are responsible to deny the flesh by no longer choosing to live for themselves. Self denial is not optional for the true disciple of Jesus. Self denial is a continuous act of the will in which we choose to come into alignment with the fact of the new creation. But without that volitional agreement, which is an act of faith in what Christ has done in making our spirit alive to God and dead to sin, we fail to align ourselves with the power of the cross. Subsequently we fall short of an experiential conformity to His death.

A Cross in our Heart

Living with the cross planted firmly in our heart is part of our conformity to the image of Christ. Jesus walked continuously in self denial by carrying His cross every minute of His life, not just on that fateful day when He carried His physical cross to Golgotha. He was crucified to the world as a permanent lifestyle. Paul said, "God forbid that I should boast except in the cross of our Lord Jesus Christ, by whom the world has been crucified to me, and I to the world" (Galatians 6:14). It is as we affirm the power of the cross in our lives that we overcome the world and all of its temptations. Jesus did this Himself because He lived as one who was dead to the world and gloriously alive to the Father.

This principle of life and death is something which needs to be firmly established in the heart of the believer because it is something permanently established in the heart of Christ and in the heart of the Father. This is a major part of what it means to be conformed to the image of Christ. To be alive to something means we must simultaneously be dead to something else. God is permanently alive to righteousness and dead to sin and unrighteousness. In that sense, the cross is a universal, cosmic reality at all moments throughout all eternity. It was acted out in time, two thousand years ago, when Christ was crucified. The work of the cross points to something even deeper in the heart of Christ.

John points to this reality in the book of Revelation when he describes Jesus as "the Lamb that was slain from the creation of the world" (Revelation 13:8 NIV). He was "the Lamb who was killed before the world was made" (NLT). The cross was inevitable in a world inhabited by human beings with a free will who were gloriously made in the image and likeness of God.

Before God began the entire project of creation, He had paid the price of the death of His Son in His own heart. He knew in advance that free will would lead to the fall and the fall would, of necessity, lead to the cross. This is why John could say that the cross was a reality in the very heart of God even before the world was made.

The cross is the ultimate symbol of this revelatory principle of death and life. Life can only exist when there is simultaneously death to something else. God Himself is alive to righteousness because He is dead to sin. God has a cross planted permanently in His heart and we, who are made in His image and likeness, must also embrace this reality. We must allow the Spirit to plant the cross as a "tree of life" in the centre of our hearts as well. The cross was an instrument of death, but Peter called it a "tree" because the cross of Christ is the key to all spiritual life and power. "He himself bore our sins in his body on the tree" (1 Peter 2:24 NIV). Jesus suffered death for all humanity in order to make way for life. In this sense, the cross becomes a tree of life! Any expression of Christianity devoid of the centrality of the cross is not an authentic expression of the Christian faith. Cross-less Christianity is no Christianity at all.

Jesus modelled a life of carrying the cross to His disciples well before His actual crucifixion. When He called upon His followers to take up their cross daily and to deny themselves, He was calling them to adopt this biblical principle of a daily lifestyle of self denial. We do this by living out the principle of the cross through which we are simultaneously dead to sin and the world and gloriously alive to God and His heart of love. Jesus called this "taking up our cross." He practiced what He preached.

Paul explained what a life looked like when the cross was planted firmly in the centre of our heart as a permanent reality. Describing what it meant in daily terms to be co-crucified with Christ, Paul spoke of, "Always carrying about in the body the dying of the Lord Jesus, that the life of Jesus also may be manifested in our body. For we who live are always delivered to death for Jesus' sake, that the life of Jesus also may be manifested in our mortal flesh. So then death is working in us, but life in you" (2 Corinthians 4:10-12).

Paul was *always carrying* the cross as a daily reality because He had said yes to the crucified life. He understood this principle of life and death. He recognised that the cross was the ultimate revelation of the wisdom and the power of God. He refused to descend into religious sophistry and trite clichés that would shift our focus away from the centrality of the cross to mere human philosophies. He could see through the religiosity of both the Greek philosophers and the Jews who, in their own unique ways, depended on alternatives to the cross to sustain and uphold their lifeless forms of religion.

Man-Made Religion versus the Cross

Paul said the "Greeks seek after wisdom; but we preach Christ crucified" (1 Corinthians 1:22). Paul deliberately preached his message, "not with wisdom of words, lest the cross of Christ should be made of no effect. For the message of the cross is foolishness to those who are perishing, but to us who are being saved it is the power of God" (1 Corinthians 1:17-18). The Greeks descended into a philosophy of spiritual sounding words to express their spiritual beliefs and ideas.

The cross, with its raw and brutal principle of death, was an offence to worldly philosophers. But it was also an offence to the Jews, who insisted that salvation was attained through the observation of external rules and laws. Paul insisted that if salvation depended upon circumcision and the observance of the law, then "the offense of the cross has ceased" (Galatians 5:11). Why is the cross an offence to humanity? It offends our minds because it runs counter to every worldly philosophy and religious system that tries to create a path to God either through empty philosophy or legalistic systems of external rules and laws.

For Paul, his own mystical union into the death and resurrection of Christ nullified every vain religious philosophy, which consisted of mere words of so-called "wisdom" and the keeping of external laws. Through the cross, God puts everything to death – all empty philosophies and external systems of rules and regulations. The cross goes right to the heart of the matter and it conquers the very power of sin by putting it to death. Surrounded as he was by Greek philosophers and Jewish legalists, Paul said, "For I determined not to know anything among you except Jesus Christ and Him crucified" (1 Corinthians 2:2).

Whenever Christianity is reduced to a system of intellectual philosophy or a system of external rules and laws, it is "emptied of its power" (1 Corinthians 1:17 NIV). The cross is only powerful when it is planted in the human heart and the believer chooses to align himself with this grand cosmic reality that transcends space and time. God shows us what it means to be dead to sin and alive to righteousness. The cross is the ultimate wisdom of God, but it is mere foolishness to those who are perishing. They will never comprehend it because it is a deep mystical reality that transcends every human religious system through which man could boast.

Paul said, "But God forbid that I should boast except in the cross of our Lord Jesus Christ" (Galatians 6:14). "Where, then, is boasting? It is excluded" (Romans 3:27 NIV). The cross nullifies every human boast of great intellectual philosophies and of complex systems of external laws and regulations. There is no salvation in the keeping of the law or in high-sounding worldly religious philosophies. The cross cuts through all of this brilliantly because it is the genius of God. It is God's supreme wisdom to exalt something as foolish as a cross through which every source of human boasting is nullified in one fell swoop.

The cross is food for the heart. It cannot be comprehended intellectually because it is a revelation that can only be embraced within the heart as we learn to live in the power of this ultimate cosmic principle. God makes every believer brand new on the inside by giving them a new spirit and a new heart. But there is an imperative for every believer to activate the reality of the new creation by saying yes to God in His passion to plant the cross in the centre of the human heart. This is a daily choice to come into alignment with what God has already done in the human spirit. This is where the battle rages, because we have been accustomed to living our entire life exclusively for ourselves.

For Paul, the historical reality that "One died for all" meant that "all died" (2 Corinthians 5:14). And because in Christ we all died, Paul insisted that we must therefore come into alignment with this reality through faith and activate the fullness of the power of the cross in our lives. "He died for all, [so] that those who live should live no longer for themselves, but for Him who died for them and rose again" (2 Corinthians 5:15). Living in the power of the cross is a day by day, moment by moment choice as we place our faith in the finished work of Christ upon the cross. The simple choice to deny ourselves and take up our cross brings our heart into perfect alignment with the reality of the new creation.

Paul said, "For if you live according to the sinful nature, you will die; but if by the Spirit you *put to death* the misdeeds of the body, you will live" (Romans 8:13 NIV). For Paul there was a present continuous obligation to put to death everything that constituted our old life. "Put to death, therefore, whatever belongs to your earthly nature: sexual immorality, impurity, lust, evil desires and greed, which is idolatry" (Colossians 3:5 NIV). There would be no such imperative to "put to death" all that constitutes our old selfish existence if God had done it all for us. God's part is to make us a new creation. Our part is to ratify and activate this reality as a daily expression of our faith. We have been crucified together with Christ but we have to make a present continuous choice to come into alignment with what God has already done in our heart. In Colossians 3:8, Paul said, "But now, *you yourselves* are to put off all these...." He then lists a number of the fruits of the flesh that we are personally responsible to put off.

> The death He [Christ] died, He died to sin once for all; but the life He lives, He lives to God. In the same way, count yourselves dead to sin but alive to God in Christ Jesus. Therefore do not let sin reign in your mortal body so that you obey its evil desires. (Romans 6:10-12 NIV)

We refuse to let sin reign in our lives by considering ourselves dead to sin in Christ. But so many Christians simply refuse to come into alignment with the power of the cross and they live their entire lives languishing under the power of sin and death even though God has performed a miracle inside their heart. Many born again believers live as though this miracle has never taken place. Therefore, they miss out on the blessing of this "newness of life" because of their stubborn refusal to embrace the cross by allowing God to establish the cross in the centre of their heart. The Spirit is continually at work within us to persuade us to say yes to the cross.

Paul said it is through the Spirit that we put to death the deeds of the old life. "If by the Spirit you **put to death** the misdeeds of the body, you will live" (Romans 8:13 NIV). The Holy Spirit continually seeks to establish the cross in our hearts. He cannot do this for us. It is a daily choice that we must make for ourselves. God has not called us to a rigorous program of self mortification, otherwise our holiness would be all about our good works and our self effort. Instead, God wants us to live by faith. Part of this faith journey is to learn how to activate what He has already done in our spirit by choice to come into full alignment in our heart and will with the finished work of Christ. This is the call to deny ourselves and take up our cross that Jesus called us to. It is all about our choices!

In this context it is noteworthy to consider Paul's use of the Greek word *apotithemi* in reference to the imperative he placed upon all who are new creations in Christ to put off [*apotithemi*] everything that constituted their old selfish and sinful life. God has made us new creations but He cannot make choices for us to put off the old nature! This is our responsibility.

- "Therefore let us cast off [*apotithemi*] the works of darkness, and let us put on the armour of light." (Romans 13:12)

- "Throw off [*apotithemi*] your old evil nature and your former way of life, which is rotten through and through, full of lust and deception." (Ephesians 4:22 NLT)

175

- "Therefore each of you must put off [*apotithemi*] falsehood and speak truthfully to his neighbour." (Ephesians 4:25 NIV)

- "But now you yourselves are to put off [*apotithemi*] all these: anger, wrath, malice, blasphemy, filthy language out of your mouth." (Colossians 3:8)

Similarly, in Hebrews we read, "Let us throw off [*apotithemi*] everything that hinders and the sin that so easily entangles, and let us run with perseverance the race marked out for us" (Hebrews 12:1 NIV). James said, "Therefore, putting aside [*apotithemi*] all filthiness and all that remains of wickedness" (James 1:21 NASB). Peter said, "Therefore, laying aside [*apotithemi*] all malice, all deceit, hypocrisy, envy, and all evil speaking" (1 Peter 2:1).

A Christian can potentially have Christ indwelling his heart for decades without ever appropriating the power of the new life if he or she is unwilling to apply the power of the cross to their old life. It is our lack of experiential conformity to the cross that hinders the release of the heart of Christ in us. The Spirit of God has declared war upon everything that has been rendered old in our lives because of the new birth. He will not rest until He has fully accomplished His mission. The nature and glory of Christ cannot be revealed in and through us until we willingly embrace the supernatural power of the cross by coming into agreement with the reality that we are now dead to sin. Living under the new dispensation of grace is the key to the transforming work of the cross. Paul outlined what it meant to live overshadowed by the empowering presence of the grace of God in Romans chapter six, where he brilliantly introduces us to a life *under grace.*

For sin shall not have dominion over you, for you are not under law but *under grace.* What then? Shall we sin because we are not under law but *under grace?* Certainly not! Do you not know that to whom you present yourselves slaves to obey, you are that one's slaves whom you obey, whether of sin leading to death, or of obedience leading to righteousness? But God be thanked that though you were slaves of sin, yet you obeyed from the heart that form of doctrine to which you were delivered. And having been set free from sin, you became slaves of righteousness. (Romans 6:14-18)

Right in the middle of Paul's revelatory epiphany of Romans chapter six he explains to us our role in activating the power of the new creation. For Paul, the grace of God empowers us through the presence of the Spirit to obey the truth and live a life of righteousness. This is how we put to death everything that constitutes our old life through the Spirit. We cannot do this in our own strength; we can only live this crucified life through the empowerment of grace. But we cannot overlook the fact that we are called to make daily choices to obey.

> For the grace of God has appeared, bringing salvation to all men, ***instructing us to deny ungodliness*** and worldly desires and to live sensibly, righteously and godly in the present age, looking for the blessed hope and the appearing of the glory of our great God and Saviour, Christ Jesus, who gave Himself for us to redeem us from every lawless deed, and to purify for Himself a people for His own possession, zealous for good deeds. (Titus 2:11-14 NASB)

Grace instructs us! God's grace, or His empowering presence, continuously instructs us to deny ungodliness and worldly desires. Living under grace is the key to living the crucified life of resurrection power. Jesus said we must deny ourselves and take up our cross. Paul said we must continuously choose to no longer live for ourselves but for God. We cannot live this supernatural life without the Spirit of grace continually empowering us to put to death our old life and to deny all ungodliness and unrighteousness. God has performed a miracle inside our hearts, but it is up to us to exercise our faith in what He has already done by bringing our heart into alignment with the power of the cross.

The more we embrace the cross, the greater the glory of the life of Christ we see manifested in our personal lives. This is the New Testament key to seeing the life of Jesus manifested in our mortal bodies. We are called to live a supernatural life, and the gateway to this glorious life is to choose daily to take up our cross in obedience to Christ and to activate the fullness of the power of the new creation. We are faced with the daily choice to either live for ourselves or to live for Christ. There are only two ways a Christian can walk in this life: we can choose to live a self-centred existence or a Christ-centred existence. This is what Paul presents to us in the book of Romans: we can choose to be a slave to sin and death or a slave to righteousness. The new creation miracle now presents us with these two options. The Spirit continually reasons with us to persuade us of the wisdom of carrying the cross as the pathway to the fullness of new life in Christ.

The majority of the body of apostolic teaching in the New Testament consists in teaching and training believers how to activate new creation realities and how to live in the power of our new life in Christ. Paul gave detailed instructions on how to appropriate the fullness of this new life. All of his epistles painstakingly address the various strongholds of the human heart that stand in the way of the unveiling of the heart of Christ through every believer. In fact, Paul said that he was in a state of spiritual travail until Christ was formed inside every true disciple of Jesus. "My little children; for whom I labour in birth again until Christ is formed in you" (Galatians 4:19). At the centre of this process is the power of the cross and the challenge set before every believer to pursue an ever deepening conformity to the death of Christ to sin.

Chapter Thirteen

The Father of Spirits

"We have had human fathers who corrected us, and we paid them respect. Shall we not much more readily be in subjection to the Father of spirits and live?"
(Hebrews 12:9)

In chapter three of this book we explored the theme of the circumcision of the heart. We saw how the book of Hebrews introduces the concept of the separation of soul and spirit. God performed this partition at the moment of new birth, dividing all that is still old from all that has been made new (Hebrews 4:12). Hebrews also shows the inability of the Old Covenant laws and regulations to make the worshipper perfect. Instead, Hebrews highlights the power of the New Covenant to make "the spirits of just men perfect" (Hebrews 12:23). As we explored in chapter eight of this book, God has made our spirits righteous in His sight by imparting His own righteousness to our human spirit. In this sense, He has brought every new creation in Christ to a place of spiritual completion [teleios] in their relationship with God. Paul says that "you are complete [teleios] in Him" (Colossians 2:10).

It is difficult not to detect the hand of Paul in the content of the book of Hebrews. Theologians point out distinct differences between the writing style of Paul and the writing style of Hebrews, sufficient to cause most commentators to reject Pauline authorship, especially because the epistle doesn't open with the typical Pauline salutation.

My personal conviction is that the book was perhaps written by someone, like Apollos, who had been significantly influenced by Paul. The last chapter (Hebrews 13) is Pauline in every way yet the body of the epistle is clearly not Pauline in style or content. We will never know this side of heaven but, nevertheless, the contribution of this book to the delineation between what God has done in our spirit and what He is still doing in our soul resonates comprehensively with Pauline thought.

A further contribution to our understanding of the soul/spirit paradigm is found in Hebrews 12:9 where we read: "Furthermore, we have had human fathers who corrected us, and we paid them respect. Shall we not much more readily be in subjection to the Father of spirits and live?" God is the Father of our human spirit because of the new creation through which He has adopted us as sons and daughters into His family. We are now eternally related to God as our Father. Nevertheless, we are exhorted in Hebrews to voluntarily bring our entire being into subjection to the Father of our spirits. This call to a life of authentic submission to our Heavenly Father brings into focus a significant aspect of our transformation from glory to glory. Let's read the entire passage:

> You have forgotten the exhortation which speaks to you as to sons: "My son, do not despise the chastening of the Lord nor be discouraged when you are rebuked by Him; for whom the Lord loves He chastens and scourges every son whom He receives." If you endure chastening God deals with you as with sons; for what son is there whom a father does not chasten? But if you are without chastening, of which all have become partakers, then you are illegitimate and not sons. Furthermore, we have had human fathers who corrected us, and we paid them respect. Shall we not much more readily

be in subjection to the Father of spirits and live? For they indeed for a few days chastened us as seemed best to them, but He for our profit, that we may be partakers of His holiness. Now no chastening seems to be joyful for the present, but painful; nevertheless, afterward it yields the peaceable fruit of righteousness to those who have been trained by it. (Hebrews 12:5-11)

We learn a number of significant truths from this important passage of Scripture. First and most importantly, we are now sons and daughters with the same family identity and status before the Father as Jesus continuously enjoys. He is not ashamed to call us "brethren" (Hebrews 2:11). Nevertheless, it is imperative that we come under the loving training of our Father if we wish to enjoy the full blessing of being "partakers of the divine nature" (2 Peter 1:4). Without this voluntary submission we will not live in the fullness of righteousness, peace, and holiness that has already been imparted to our spirit. The key to abundant life is in subjecting ourselves fully to the discipline of the Father. The promise is that if we comprehensively submit ourselves to Him, we shall be fully alive. Jesus has promised us life in all of its fullness!

Training in Righteousness and Holiness

The missing ingredient that brings believers into the experiential reality of who we already are as new creations is the training process through which the Father disciplines and trains every adopted son and daughter. At the centre of this training, as we saw in the previous chapter, is the power of the cross. Our training under the Father is "cross-training." Holiness is a gift from God. Christ is our holiness yet, we must be willing to enter into training in order to experientially partake of His holiness in every area of our interior life. Our Heavenly Father chastens us "for our profit, that we may be partakers of His holiness" (Hebrews 10:9-10). This holiness is not attained through works, but through a disciplined life of faith, obedience, and self-control. As we learn how to live and abide in the free gift of Christ's holiness, we "put to death" every remaining vestige of the old selfish nature, wherever it has contaminated the soul.

It is one thing to be a new creation, but it is an entirely different reality to be a true overcomer who enjoys the fullness of the new life in Christ. In order to enter into this advanced state of spiritual blessing we must submit to the ongoing process of the purification of the soul. The Bible reveals that there is an ongoing purging or refining from residual sin in the soul of the believer. Malachi prophesied of the coming of the Messiah who would sit as a "Refiner's Fire:"

> See, I will send My messenger, who will prepare the way before Me. Then suddenly the Lord you are seeking will come to His temple; the Messenger of the Covenant, whom you desire, will come," says the Lord Almighty. "But who can endure the day of His coming? Who can stand when He appears? For He will be like a Refiner's Fire or a launderer's soap. He will sit as a refiner and purifier of silver; He will purify the Levites and refine them like gold and silver." (Malachi 3:1-3)

God prophetically promised that the saints of the New Covenant would be experientially purified and refined. "Many will be purged, purified, and refined, but the wicked will act wickedly" (Daniel 12:10). In the New Testament, God is revealed as a "consuming fire" who has come to consume all sin and unrighteousness in His people. "God is not an indifferent bystander. He's actively cleaning house, torching all that needs to burn, and He won't quit until it's all cleansed. God Himself is Fire!" (Hebrews 12:28-29 MSG).

This refining work of God is a progressive purging and purifying of every trace of sin and selfishness from the human heart. God's intent is "to purify for Himself a people that are His very own" (Titus

2:14), no matter how long the process takes in each of our lives. The goal is a complete conformity to the image of Christ. This necessitates not only the purging of sinful behaviour, but also the purging of every vestige of self centeredness so that we live in the fullness of the self-sacrificial love of Christ. Paul discussed the necessity of this ongoing purification of the soul using the metaphor of leaven or yeast, which is notorious for its propensity to permeate the entire lump of dough.

> Do you not know that a little leaven leavens the whole lump? Therefore purge out the old leaven, that you may be a new lump, since you truly are unleavened. For indeed Christ, our Passover, was sacrificed for us. Therefore let us keep the feast, not with old leaven, nor with the leaven of malice and wickedness, but with the unleavened bread of sincerity and truth. (1 Corinthians 5:6-8)

In this passage the paradox of sanctification stares us in the face. Paul exhorts us to purge out the old leaven because we are already unleavened. What does he mean by this classic paradox? The answer lies in the fact that your spirit has been comprehensively unleavened but your soul is still leavened. That is why there is a biblical imperative to pursue a deeper purging and purification of the soul. In the same epistle Paul accused the Corinthians of still being carnal even though He was addressing them as genuine believers and as saints.

> And I, brethren, could not speak to you as to spiritual people but as to carnal, as to babes in Christ. I fed you with milk and not with solid food; for until now you were not able to receive it, and even now you are still not able; for you are still carnal. For where there are envy, strife, and divisions among you, are you not carnal and behaving like mere men? For when one says, "I am of Paul," and another, "I am of Apollos," are you not carnal? (1 Corinthians 3:1-4)

Paul described these born again believers as "carnal" or *sarkikos* in Greek. *Sarkikos* is derived from the root word *sarx,* which means "*flesh.*" Paul was describing many of the Corinthians as fleshly, still under the sway of their old selfish nature. That is why he passionately exhorted them to purge out the old leaven so that they may become a comprehensively new "lump," free of the old leaven of malice and wickedness. Our spirit has already been purified of the leaven of sin and wickedness but our soul experiences a progressive cleansing and purification.

It is through this purity that we can commune with a Holy God, spirit to Spirit. Purity is a free gift from God and is characterised by the complete washing away of all impurity. But there is a difference between purity and maturity. We may be pure yet immature. Maturity is a sustained and comprehensive purity. A mature believer has been trained by Christ to walk in a sustained experiential purity in every area of their soul. A brand new believer can immediately identify purity but it is only as he or she grows up into maturity that this purity is sustained in such a manner that the saint walks continuously in righteousness and true holiness in every part of their mind, will, and emotions. In this way, the holiness that the believer tastes in his spiritual infancy and immaturity is extended to touch and permeate every part of his mind, his will, and his emotions, progressively freeing him from every trace of selfishness. "And everyone who has this hope in Him purifies himself, just as He is pure" (1 John 3:3). All the New Testament writers attest to this ongoing purification of the soul.

God is training us to live and abide in the fullness of Christ. Jesus said, "A disciple is not above his teacher, but everyone who is perfectly trained will be like his teacher" (Luke 6:40). Only those who embrace the training and discipline of the Lord grow up into full experiential Christlikeness. Those who are fully trained have become mature in Christ. On the one hand, the Father trains His sons and daughters, yet on the other hand, we are also instructed to train ourselves.

"But solid food is for the mature, who by constant use *have trained* themselves to distinguish good from evil. Therefore let us leave the elementary teachings about Christ and go on to maturity" (Hebrews 5:14-6:1). The key to Christian maturity is the training process through which we are trained to live continuously in the purity and holiness of Christ, which is given to us as a free gift.

All believers are to be brought up "in the training and admonition of the Lord" (Ephesians 6:4). This training is essential for every believer. Paul said, "Everyone who competes in the games goes into strict training. They do it to get a crown that will not last; but we do it to get a crown that will last forever" (1 Corinthians 9:25 NIV). "All athletes practice strict self-control" (NLT). Leaders in the church are instructed to facilitate this training process in order to actively train and disciple believers to live a life of holiness. "All Scripture is God-breathed and is useful for teaching, rebuking, correcting, and *training in righteousness*" (2 Timothy 3:16 NIV).

Train Yourself

Paul said, "Train yourself to be godly. For physical training is of some value, but godliness has value for all things, holding promise for both the present life and the life to come" (1 Timothy 4:7-8 NIV). We are to train ourselves to be godly. The Greek word for "godly" is *eusebeia,* which, according to the Strong's concordance, is a synonym for holiness. It is powerfully juxtaposed against ungodliness [asebeia] or sinfulness. Here, Paul is advocating the active pursuit of a holy life through rigorous spiritual training under the loving guidance of the Father. Jerry Bridges, in his book, *The Practice of Godliness,* explains the relationship between godliness and holiness.

> God is infinitely perfect in His holiness. Not the slightest degree of sin taints His character. To be Godlike in our character, then, is first of all to be holy. The practice of godliness

involves the pursuit of holiness. If we want to train ourselves to be godly, it must be holiness in every area of our lives![20]

So when Paul exhorts us to train ourselves to be godly, he is actually exhorting us to train ourselves to walk in the holiness of the Lord. Every Christian ought to be in training to live in the fullness of the gift of righteousness, purity, and holiness. Godliness, righteousness, and holiness are virtues to be actively pursued by all believers. "But you, O man of God, flee these things [greed and the love of money] and pursue righteousness, godliness, faith, love, patience, gentleness" (1 Timothy 6:11).

We are commanded to pursue righteousness, godliness, and holiness: "Pursue peace with all people, and holiness, without which no one will see the Lord" (Hebrews 12:14). Holiness is a gift, yet paradoxically it is something that we are commanded to pursue. Through the grace of God we enter into a life of discipline, self-control, and training in order to learn how to deny ungodliness and worldly lusts. In the previous chapter we considered the following passage in the book of Titus. Let's take a look at it again in the light of the call to train ourselves in order to enter into the fullness of godliness and holiness.

> For the grace of God that brings salvation has appeared to all men. It teaches us to say 'No' to ungodliness and worldly passions, and to live self-controlled, upright and godly lives in this present age, while we wait for the blessed hope; the glorious appearing of our great God and Saviour, Jesus Christ, who gave himself for us to redeem us from all wickedness and to purify for himself a people that are his very own, eager to do what is good. These, then, are the things you should teach. Encourage and rebuke with all authority. (Titus 2:11-15 NIV)

This training process, through which we learn to deny ungodliness and to cultivate godliness, extends to every part of our interior lives and even to the management of our physical bodies. Paul said that God is active in the lives of His sons and daughters to purify for Himself a people who have been purged of all wickedness. This purging only takes place as we learn to say "No" to all ungodliness in our lives.

The Art of Self-Training

One of the fruits of the Holy Spirit in our lives is self-control. Self-control featured strongly in Paul's theology. Luke tells us that Paul "discoursed on righteousness, self-control and the judgment to come" (Acts 24:25 NIV). Paul exhorted Christians to "continue in faith, love, and holiness, with self-control" (1 Timothy 2:15). Self-control is an intrinsic part of training in righteousness and holiness. A self-controlled Christian brings every aspect of their soul life into subjection to their spirit in order to establish internal spiritual government.

We are instructed to put off the old selfish life and to bring it into subjection to the Holy Spirit. Selfishness is deeply ingrained in human beings and it does not disappear straight away. If it did, the whole world would be saved by now. Imagine if every Christian was comprehensively delivered from all selfishness the moment they were born again. What a glorious witness that would be to the world. But instead, we must intentionally confront every trace of self-will and self-centred thinking and behaviour. To walk consistently in the Spirit means living a thoroughly Christ-centred life that puts off the old selfish way of life in order to be filled with the self-sacrificial agape love of Christ. This is the pathway of taking up our cross.

God is seeking to free us from ourselves and all the consequences of a self centered existence. Paul understood the flesh as the old "self" life with "self" still seated upon the throne. "For Christ's love compels us, because we are convinced that one died for all, and therefore all died. And He died for all, that those who live should no longer live for themselves but for him who died for them and was raised again" (2 Corinthians 5:14-15 NIV). Paul used the language of refusing to live for our old self anymore.

> We should *not trust in ourselves* but in God who raises the dead. (2 Corinthians 1:9)

> We who are strong ought to bear with the failings of the weak and *not to please ourselves*. (Romans 15:1 NIV)

Human beings are fundamentally selfish. Left to themselves, they are greedy, self-centered, self-willed, self-obsessed, and filled only with self-love and self-interest. The old sinful nature runs much deeper than a mere list of sinful behaviors that we are called to turn away from. Redefining "the flesh" as a self-centered existence expands the frontiers of what it means to live and walk in the Spirit. A person who truly walks in the Spirit must be free from the dictates of all selfishness. Paul spoke of sinful humanity in terms of their selfishness and their inability to love others and exercise true self-control.

> You should also know this Timothy, that in the last days there will be very difficult times. For people will love only themselves and their money. They will be boastful and proud, scoffing at God, disobedient to their parents, and ungrateful. They will consider nothing sacred. They will be unloving and unforgiving; they will slander others and have no self-control; they will be cruel and have no interest in what is good. They will betray their friends, be reckless, be puffed up with pride, and love pleasure rather than God. (2 Timothy 3:1-4 NLT)

Jesus also confronted the bankruptcy of the self-life:

> Speaking to the people, He went on, "Take care! Protect yourself against the least bit of greed. Life is not defined by what you have, even when you have a lot." Then he told them this story: "The farm of a certain rich man produced a terrific crop. He talked to himself: 'What can I do? My barn isn't big enough for this harvest.' Then he said, 'Here's what I'll do: I'll tear down my barns and build bigger ones. Then I'll gather in all my grain and goods, and I'll say to myself, "Self, you've done well! You've got it made and can now retire. Take it easy and have the time of your life!"' Just then God showed up and said, "Fool! Tonight you will die. And your barnful of goods—who gets it?" That's what happens when you fill your barn with self and not with God. (Luke 12:15- 21 MSG)

Ouch! Eugene Peterson, the author of The Message Bible, zeroed in on the stronghold of human selfishness as the essence of sin.

Jesus Calls us to a Lifestyle of Radical Self Denial

We understand that the Father is training us as we are also called to train ourselves. This is where we connect the lifestyle of self-control and self denial with taking up our cross. "If anyone desires to come after Me, let him deny himself, and take up his cross daily, and follow Me" (Luke 9:23). "If any of you wants to be my follower, you must put aside your selfish ambition, shoulder your cross daily, and follow me" (NLT).

We are called to consistently deny the claims of the old selfish existence every day of our lives. "For whoever desires to save his life will lose it, but whoever loses his life for My sake and the gospel's will save it" (Mark 8:35). Once again, the Message Bible paraphrases this verse as: "Self-help is no help at all. Self-sacrifice is the way: My way, to saving yourself, your true self" (Mark 8:35). The "free" version of you is a person living free from all selfishness. The Message Bible translation exposes this selfish old nature with self on the throne.

> Among those who belong to Christ, everything connected with getting our own way is killed off for good – crucified! (Galatians 5:24)

> So don't you see that we don't owe this old do-it-yourself life one red cent. There's nothing in it for us, nothing at all. The best thing to do is give it a decent burial and get on with your new life. (Romans 8:12-13)

God is systematically purging every son and daughter of selfishness and the fruit of selfishness, which is sin. He trains us by exposing and confronting every expression of selfishness, calling us to deeper repentance and a self-sacrificial lifestyle of love. Paul instructed us to put to death the old selfish nature and to cleanse ourselves of every trace of the self life. This is the art of self-control that every believer is learning as they step more and more into becoming a true disciple and follower of Christ. The entire New Testament advocates a self imposed course of intensive spiritual training where we play an active role in putting off the old self life.

In addition to the adoption of this self-imposed process of training for godliness and holiness, God the Father also actively trains and disciples His children through a process of exhortation, encouragement, correction, rebuke, and discipline in order that we may become experiential partakers of His free gift of holiness. He speaks to us through His Spirit in order to train us in the things that please Him and the things that displease Him. We are the branches attached to the vine, and the Father is the vinedresser. He prunes the branches in order to bring forth greater spiritual fruitfulness. According to the book of Hebrews, He trains us so that we will consistently be partakers of His holiness. This is what it really means to abide in the vine: to remain in Christ's self-sacrificial love.

Pastoral Training in Righteousness

The Father disciplines and chastens His sons and daughters. Similarly, Jesus says, "As many as I love, I rebuke and chasten. Therefore be zealous and repent" (Revelation 3:19). Jesus rebukes, chastens, and disciplines the church in order to train her to live in the fullness of His holiness. The epistles of Paul (in particular 1 Corinthians) and the letters of Jesus to the seven churches in the book of Revelation are powerful examples of the Father training His people to live in the fullness of the righteousness and holiness of Christ. Both Jesus and Paul target strongholds of ungodliness, selfishness, and deception, calling the people of God to deeper repentance and to turn away from idolatry, pride, and sexual immorality. This is the Father chastening and disciplining His children so that they will enter into a fuller and deeper participation in His holiness.

In like manner, Jesus painstakingly taught and trained His disciples, walking them through many lessons concerning authentic freedom from the self-life. They did not get free of their foolish and carnal mindsets right away. They were self-willed and sometimes stubborn in their unbelief, but Jesus continued to pastor them and systematically train them to live in true freedom from the dictates of the flesh. He is always calling us to live in the free version of ourselves. He does this by giving us prophetic glimpses into who it is that we are becoming as we embrace the call to purify ourselves, just as He is pure. We must fix our eyes on Jesus to continually remind ourselves of what true freedom really looks like.

Our Father is training us, and we are instructed to train ourselves to live in righteousness and true holiness. Between the Father's commitment to train us and our deepening commitment to train ourselves to live in purity and holiness, the end result is a growing conformity to the holiness and selflessness of Jesus. We are changed from glory to glory as we fix our eyes on Jesus our example. As the writer to the Hebrews says, His discipline is all "for our profit, that we may be partakers of His holiness. Now no chastening seems to be joyful for the present, but painful; nevertheless, afterward it yields the peaceable fruit of righteousness to those who have been trained by it" (Hebrews 12:10-11).

In 1 Corinthians, Paul recommends a lifestyle of careful self examination as the higher path; whenever we choose to neglect this lifestyle of self discipline, we set ourselves up for the discipline of the Father.

> A man ought to examine himself before he eats of the bread and drinks of the cup. For anyone who eats and drinks without recognizing the body of the Lord eats and drinks judgment on himself. That is why many among you are weak and sick, and a number of you have fallen asleep. But if we judged ourselves, we would not come under judgment. When we are judged by the Lord, we are being disciplined so that we will not be condemned with the world. (1 Corinthians 11:28-32 NIV)

God's judgment of His sons and daughters is really His discipline. Paul is careful in this passage to define what he means by God's judgment. It is not ultimate judgment, it is an evaluation of our behaviour. Paul's point is that we only come under the discipline of the Father when we fail to discipline and train ourselves. The higher path is to judge, or evaluate, our own conduct to discern whether we are being motivated by sin or selfishness. But if we neglect to judge ourselves, we set ourselves up for our loving Father to intervene. When He intervenes, He disciplines us by correcting and rebuking us so that we come in line once again with His righteousness and holiness. This is an expression of His love.

Peter said, "For the time has come for judgment to begin at the house of God; and if it begins with us first, what will be the end of those who do not obey the gospel of God?" (1 Peter 4:17). The Father loves His children enough to correct them and rebuke them if they go astray into sin and selfishness. Paul said, "When we are judged by the Lord, we are being disciplined."

Our Father's loving judgment only comes upon His household when we reject the higher path of self evaluation and self discipline. Whenever the Father has to step in with correction or discipline, He addresses the issue that we are failing to come to terms with by ourselves. Sometimes this discipline may come through our friends speaking into our lives, because we are suffering from a "blind spot" where we are not seeing the consequences of our own actions.

This external discipline is not joyful, but painful; nevertheless it yields the peaceable fruit of righteousness and holiness. If we would judge ourselves, we would not come under the Father's judgment. So the moral of the story is that we embrace the higher path of self evaluation in order to avoid getting tapped on the shoulder by our Father. The Father only disciplines us so we may truly live. As we come into subjection to the Father of spirits, we enter into the fullness of life that Jesus promised. Jesus said, "My purpose is to give life in all its fullness" (John 10:10 NLT).

Chapter Fourteen

Establishing Internal
Spiritual Government

Every born again believer must learn how to train their body, mind, will, and emotions to come into subjection to their spirit. Graham Cooke highlights how important it is for our spirit man, joined to the Holy Spirit, to learn how to govern over every part of our inner being.

> The inner man, the spirit, wears the outer man, the soul and the body. To be effective for Christ, we must release the inner man. To be fulfilled and joyful, the spirit must govern the soul. We are our own worst enemy, by refusing to subject our soul to our spirit. If we allow our spirit to govern the way we act ... we will have God's empowerment.[21]

There is an internal governmental order that God seeks to establish in the heart of every believer. Paul taught that God has joined His Spirit to our human spirit. "He who is joined to the Lord is one spirit with Him" (1 Corinthians 6:17). This revelation is the first step toward establishing an internal government of the Spirit. Paul established this principle of internal government when he described the Spirit as the Lord Himself. "Now the Lord is the Spirit and where the Spirit of the Lord is; there is freedom" (2 Corinthians 3:17 NIV). The

Lord is the Spirit! Since the Spirit is Lord, it means that your human spirit has been supernaturally joined to the Lord Himself. As Lord, He seeks to establish His Lordship over every part of our being: our mind, will, emotions, and body so that each part is firmly under the governance of the Spirit of the Lord who is supernaturally joined to our spirit.

"Of the increase of His government there shall be no end" (Isaiah 9:7). Of course, this applies to the expansion of the kingdom government of Jesus throughout the entire earth, but it also speaks to the issue of the internal spiritual government of King Jesus being established in the heart of every believer. Consider for a moment all the interior territory that God wants to bring under the government of the Spirit. He wants to bring every thought captive to the obedience of Christ. He wants to bring every single aspect of our will into a perfect synergy and alignment with His will. Jesus modelled this when He said, "Not my will but Yours be done" (Luke 22:42).

God also wants to deliver us from every negative and destructive emotion that seeks to reign within the human soul, so that all of our emotions are governed by the Spirit. Jesus modelled emotional wholeness because His emotions were always subordinated to His spirit. He was never ruled by His emotions and none of His decisions were emotionally based. He lived for the will of God rather than the dictates of His own subjective feelings. God seeks to reign over every bodily appetite so that the body, with its own set of physical drives and passions, does not set the agenda for how we live our personal lives. God has a higher agenda to bring our mind, will, emotions, and physical being under the reign of the Lordship of Jesus.

It doesn't take a great deal of imagination to think about what our lives would look like, as believers in Jesus, if we were to allow the desires of the body to reign unchecked and unrestrained by our spirit. Similarly, our thought life, if left to run wild and unconstrained by the rule and reign of our spirit, would lead to all manner of carnal, perverse, and selfish thoughts. Likewise, if our emotions are not under the rule of our spirit and they were left to rule over us, we would be emotional basket cases! Whenever our will is out of alignment with the perfect will of God something will always go wrong inside of our hearts. A person who is controlled by their bodily lusts and appetites will quickly descend into the abyss of carnality and inevitable spiritual ruin. There can be no doubt that God intends our human spirit, supernaturally joined to God's Holy Spirit, to rule and exercise lordship over our body and our soul. This is God's internal order for every human being.

Jesus perfectly modelled this kind of life when He lived upon the earth. His human spirit was in perfect spiritual union with the Spirit of the Father and it was completely under the rule and reign of the Spirit of the Lord. In this permanent state, His spirit exercised total control and governance over all four theatres of battle: the mind, the will, the emotions, and the body. Whilst Jesus endured temptation, and sometimes even perhaps extreme temptation, He never yielded to sin and was able to walk in perfect internal order through the empowerment of the Holy Spirit. His mind, His will, His emotions, and the desires of His own physical body were continually under the direct control and influence of the Spirit.

Jesus was a Father-pleaser! He could faithfully say; "I always do those things that please Him" (John 8:29). This life of perfect internal government was sustained and made possible through the indwelling of the Spirit of God who kept Jesus in a state of perfect spiritual freedom and grace. Jesus modelled the reality that there is a place in the Spirit where we can live a life of glorious internal government, where our spirit is restored to its rightful place of rulership over all four areas where the battle rages. This doesn't mean that we will not experience temptation, but Paul insisted that as new creations in Christ, God has always provided a way of escape. "No temptation has overtaken you except such as is common to man; but God is faithful, who will not allow you to be tempted beyond what you are able, but with the temptation will also make the way of escape, that you may be able to bear it" (1 Corinthians 10:13).

The work of the Holy Spirit inside the heart of every believer is to establish this internal spiritual government where every area of our interior lives are brought back into divine order. This is what it means to be conformed to the image of Christ. To move forward in this direction, every aspect of our mind, will, emotions, and physical body needs to be brought into a state of perfect alignment with the cross of Christ. We spoke in a previous chapter of the necessity of the cross being firmly planted in the centre of every human heart just as it has been eternally established within the heart of God Himself. When the cross is established over our thought life, over our emotional life, over our volitional life, and over our physical being, we live in a state of glorious experiential participation in the very life of God.

Paul said, "To be carnally minded is death but to be spiritually minded is life and peace" (Romans 8:6). We could take this same principle and apply it to the other three arenas of battle.

- "To be controlled by destructive and negative emotions is death, but to bring our emotions into subjection to the Spirit is life and peace!"

- "To be controlled by selfish choices is death, but to bring our will into perfect alignment with the Spirit is life and peace!"

- "To be controlled by the appetites of the body is death, but to bring our carnal desires under the rule and reign of the Spirit is life and peace!"

This issue is a matter of life or death! When an aspect of our internal life is brought into alignment with the power of the cross, we experience the blessing of the flow of the very life of God in our heart. Paul said, "Our spirit is alive because of righteousness." Our spirit man is brimming with resurrection life. When our mind, our will, and our emotions are aligned with our spirit, we experience life in all its fullness.

The issue is a matter of control. Who is in control of our interior life? When we are Spirit-controlled, we experience inner life and peace. "Of the increase of His government ***and peace*** there will be no end" (Isaiah 9:7). God rules in righteousness and peace, and the fruit of righteousness shall be peace and joy forever. "The kingdom of God is ... righteousness, peace and joy in the Holy Spirit" (Romans 14:17). The Spirit-controlled life is the pathway to true life, peace, and joy.

The Spirit-Controlled Life

A truly Spirit-filled existence describes a life where God establishes the government of the Holy Spirit in every part of our soul. For someone to be truly Spirit-filled in a sustained manner, like Jesus was, they must learn how to establish strong internal government and to allow everything that is true of their renewed human spirit to spill over into their soul so that their mind, will, and emotions are comprehensively permeated and ruled by the Spirit of the Lord. The Spirit-filled life is really the "Spirit-controlled life!"

As we saw in a previous chapter, Kenneth Wuest, in his *Expanded Translation of the Greek New Testament,* chose to translate every reference to the "Spirit-filled life" as the "Spirit controlled life." "Stop being intoxicated with wine, in which state of intoxication there is profligacy. But be constantly *controlled* by the Spirit" (Ephesians 5:18 Wuest). His point was that if someone was truly filled with the Holy Spirit, just as Jesus was filled with the Holy Spirit, they would have to exhibit a life that was comprehensively permeated and governed by the Spirit who is both "Lord" and "Holy." Paul called the Holy Spirit the "Spirit of holiness" in Romans 1:4. To be truly filled with the

Holy Spirit, someone must be living under the influence of the Spirit of Holiness and the Lordship of Christ in every area of their soul.

There is never a question about the holy or sanctified state of the regenerated human spirit because, as we saw in a previous chapter, our spirit has already been Spirit filled. Paul said, "You have been given fullness in Christ" (Colossians 2:10 NIV). Our human spirit is thoroughly and comprehensively immersed in God's Holy Spirit. However, God wants this Spirit-filled state to extend to every aspect of our soul. He wants this fullness to overflow out of our innermost being and to thoroughly pervade every aspect of our soul, permeating every part of our mind, will, and emotions, just like Jesus. "For He satisfies the longing soul and fills the hungry soul with goodness" (Psalm 107:9).

In church circles we glibly toss around the term "Spirit-filled" as though it was an identification tag for our denominational affiliation. But when this term is reduced to a descriptor of our church background, we cheapen and diminish a glorious New Testament concept. It is not an affiliation to a Pentecostal or Charismatic church, but a state of spiritual existence where the Spirit of the Lord has established a strong internal government over both spirit and soul.

You are not Spirit-filled because you attend a Pentecostal or Charismatic church! You are gloriously Spirit-filled when every sphere of your soul and your body are under the rule and reign of the Lordship of Jesus Christ. "And having prayed, the place in which they were gathered was shaken. And they were all controlled by the Holy Spirit and went to speaking the word of God with fearless confidence and freedom of speech" (Acts 4:31 Wuest). Someone who is comprehensively controlled by the Holy Spirit is going to look a lot like Jesus. "He who says he abides in Him ought himself also to walk just as He walked" (1 John 2:6).

I like to think in visual terms. If we visualise our human spirit as a cylinder located within a larger cylinder, it helps us to develop a picture of the fullness of the Spirit in our human spirit overflowing into our soul, which is represented by the outer cylinder. The inner cylinder is completely full of God, and it is intended to overflow in such a way that it comprehensively fills the outer cylinder. Jesus promised that "rivers of living water" would flow from our innermost being. "He who believes in Me," as the Scripture said, "From his innermost being will flow rivers of living water" (John 7:38 NASB). God wants the river of life to overflow from our spirit into every part of our soul. This water of life can rise to such an extent that our soul is filled to the point of overflowing. This is what the Scriptures mean in their exhortation to be continuously filled with the Holy Spirit.

Controlling our Bodies

A Spirit-filled believer is someone who has learnt to bring everything within them into subjection to the Holy Spirit. Paul taught the necessity of bringing our physical bodies into subjection to the Spirit, "Just as you used to offer the parts of your body in slavery to impurity and to ever-increasing wickedness, so now offer them in slavery to righteousness leading to holiness" (Romans 6:19 NIV). Paul said, "I discipline my body like an athlete, training it to do what it should" (1 Corinthians 9:27 NLT). We are under obligation to learn how to control our physical bodies with their rampant desires for food, physical slothfulness, and sexual gratification. Paul instructed the believers in the church of Thessalonica:

> It is God's will that you should be sanctified: that you should avoid sexual immorality; that each of you should learn to **control** his own body in a way that is holy and honourable, not in passionate lust like the heathen, who do not know God; for God did not call us to be impure, but to live a holy life. Therefore, he who rejects this instruction does not reject man but God, who gives you His Holy Spirit. (1 Thessalonians 4:3-5, 7 NIV)

Our spirit is already completely sanctified but our bodies are being sanctified as we bring them under the rule and reign of the Holy Spirit. We are to learn how to subdue and train our physical bodies. But this training also extends to the mind, the will, and the emotions.

Concerning the training of the mind, Paul wrote:

Finally, brothers, whatever is true, whatever is noble, whatever is right, whatever is pure, whatever is lovely, whatever is admirable – if anything is excellent or praiseworthy – think about such things. Whatever you have learned or received or heard from me, or seen in me – put it into practice. And the God of peace will be with you. (Philippians 4:8-9 NIV)

We are to so train our minds that we "take captive every thought to make it obedient to Christ" (2 Corinthians 10:5). Similarly, we are to train our will to bring it into subjection to the will of God and we are to train our emotions so that our emotions are subjected to our spirit. The alternative is to allow our emotions to rule over our spirit and that is never a pretty sight. The goal of our personal training is always to bring every part of our being under the rule and reign of the Spirit. In so doing, we extend God's government and peace to every aspect of our interior life. Every believer must carry a vision for bringing every part of their lives under the rule and control of our human spirit who is joined to the Holy Spirit.

Supernatural Self-control

In Acts 24:25, Paul reasoned with Felix about righteousness and self-control. In Paul's mind there was an intimate relationship between the two. Our spirit has been made righteous but we must learn the art of practicing self-control if we truly desire to live experientially in the righteousness of God. Paul distinguished between righteousness as a gift and righteousness as a lifestyle. Our regenerated spirit is comprehensively righteous, but our soul must be systematically conformed to righteousness. Paul called this process "training in righteousness" (2 Timothy 3:16 NIV). He taught that the devil is only able to tempt someone who lacks self-control (1 Corinthians 7:25). So if we want to live a life beyond the struggle of continually falling into temptation, we must learn how to walk in true self-control.

We discussed in the previous chapter that self-control is listed by Paul as one of the fruits of the Spirit in Galatians 5:23. This relationship between the practice of self-control and the gift of the Holy Spirit needs to be clearly understood. Paul appears to be communicating the idea that a person cannot walk in real self-control apart from the indwelling presence of the Holy Spirit. It is the Spirit who lives within us who empowers us to exercise self-control. Paul said that believers need to be taught how to "exercise self-control" (Titus 2:2). He is obviously not talking about natural self-control. Every human being knows how to exercise a measure of self-control in certain social settings, even in an unregenerate state. The fact that Paul's concept of self-control is rooted in the empowering of the Holy Spirit reveals that he is talking about a supernatural expression of self-control.

Any person without the Spirit can exercise a measure of natural self control. People can give up smoking, they can in some instances overcome addictions, they can restrain themselves from profanities and blasphemy, and they can control themselves in social settings sufficiently to convey a sense of moral decency. But when Paul describes Spirit empowered self-control he is moving into territory that is entirely impossible without the supernatural empowerment of the Holy Spirit.

Supernatural self-control deals with the very root of sin in our lives and brings it under the power of the cross so as to activate, by faith, the reality of what it means to be dead to sin and alive to God in every area of our soul. This kind of supernaturally empowered self-control delivers us from the very essence of our old self and liberates us to live in the reality of our new self in Christ! Paul said that "we should no longer live for ourselves but for Him" (2 Corinthians 5:15). This is clearly an entirely different kind of self-control that only comes about through the empowering of the Spirit. This is the control and subjugation of the old self life at the deepest level of our being!

Clearly, in Paul's mind there was a relationship between the power of the cross and the exercise of self-control. In Romans 8, Paul said that it is through the Spirit that we "put to death" the deeds of the body (Romans 8:13). Self-control for those who are in Christ and who have received the free gift of righteousness is not in any way the same as the unregenerate person seeking to exercise self-control in their own strength. Self-control for the believer is intertwined with the activation of the power of the cross, through our faith in the finished work of Christ. It is only through the cross that we can live a victorious life over sin and temptation.

The Pauline Paradox

You may or may not have noticed a paradox in Paul's teaching concerning the old self. In the epistle to the Colossians, Paul says we have already put off our old self through the new birth. "Do not lie to each other, since you have **taken off** your old self with its practices and **have put on** the new self, which is being renewed in knowledge in the image of its Creator (Colossians 3:9-10 NIV). Notice the tense that Paul writes in: You **have taken off** your old self and **have already put on** the new self. This is in agreement with his statement in Romans 6 where he says, "For we know that our old self **was** crucified with him so that the body of sin might be done away with" (Romans 6:6 NIV). But here is the paradox: in Ephesians, Paul uses present tense language to describe this process of experientially putting off everything that constitutes the old life.

You were taught, with regard to your former way of life, *to put off* your old self, which is being corrupted by its deceitful desires; to be made new in the attitude of your minds and *to put on* the new self, created to be like God in true righteousness and holiness. Therefore each of you **must put off** falsehood and speak truthfully to his neighbour. (Ephesians 4:22-25 NIV)

How are we to reconcile this paradox? The first statement in Colossians describes the state of our regenerated spirit now that we have been born again. The old self has already been crucified and we are now dead to sin in our spirit. This is the cutting away of the old sinful nature. "In him you were also circumcised, in the putting off of the sinful nature" (Colossians 2:11 NIV). But in Ephesians Paul is addressing the experiential application of this reality in the life of our soul. He stressed the present continuous imperative to put off everything that constituted our old life. At the centre of this process of the purification of the soul is the role of Spirit-empowered self-control. Without this control over the old self with its passions and desires we cannot enjoy the fullness of our new life in Christ.

Self-control establishes us in righteousness and holiness. Paul taught that even though our spirit is already holy, our soul must be established in holiness. "May the Lord make you increase and abound in love to one another and to all, just as we do to you, so that He may establish your hearts blameless in holiness before our God and Father" (1 Thessalonians 3:12-13). "Therefore, having these promises, beloved, let us cleanse ourselves from all filthiness of the flesh and spirit, *perfecting holiness* in the fear of God" (2 Corinthians 7:1). Holiness is perfected in us as we cultivate the art of Spirit empowered self-control, bringing every part of our mind, will, and emotions under the internal government of the Holy Spirit. In Romans 6, Paul talked about bringing our bodies into alignment with our spirit in such a way that "leads to holiness" (Romans 6:19).

No one can do this for us, not even God. We must take back, one victory at a time, every square inch of territory that the devil has stolen from us. No territory is recovered without contention. The devil contends to hold us in captivity. Therefore we must contend to wrestle that territory back from his dominion. God celebrates the process as we learn how to become overcomers and systematically take new territory in our hearts. We have to choose to bring every area of our soul into alignment with God, one choice at a time. We must choose to bring every thought into captivity to Christ one step at a time. And we must choose to bring our emotions into subjection to our spirit so that they do not run rampant. The alternative is to be ruled by our feelings, our un-renewed thought life, and our physical desires.

Self-control is the key to bringing our soul into alignment with our spirit. The soul is the battlefield. It is caught in the crossfire of a great spiritual battle between the Spirit of the Lord and "the prince of the power of the air, the *spirit* who now works in the sons of disobedience" (Ephesians 2:2). The Spirit of Christ and the "spirit of the Anti-Christ" (1 John 4:3) both contend for dominion over our soul; both spirits seek to energise and control the soul. Paul taught that there is a satanic spirit who *works* in those who are disobedient. The Greek word he used for "works" was *energeo*. Our soul can be energised either by God or by the powers of darkness. Walking in true self-control ensures that we maintain a life of obedience to God, thus keeping us free from demonic infiltration and energization. The truth is, we are continually energised either by the Spirit of Christ or the spirit of the anti-Christ. Living in the midst of a spiritual battleground ensures there can be no neutrality. God has a will for our lives, but the enemy also has a will for our lives. Whenever our will is not aligned to the will of the Lord, we inadvertently end up doing the will of the enemy, which is to be "self-willed." The same is true for our thought life. Every thought that has not been brought into captivity to obedience to Christ is a thought that is in agreement with the enemy whose agenda is to keep us disengaged from the mind of Christ. Self-centred, carnal thoughts are fertile ground for demonic energization. As long as our minds are not fixed on Christ, the enemy is delighted.

The Senses of the Soul

Our souls are inextricably linked to the sensory realm. Our five natural senses of sight, hearing, touch, taste, and smell feed a continual stream of data into our mind and our emotions. All of our natural senses are physical in nature. We see with our physical eyes; we hear with our physical ears; we taste with our physical taste buds, smell with our noses, and feel through the physical sense of touch. We are holistic beings, and our souls are housed within our physical bodies. The inextricable relationship between body and soul explains Paul's use of the Greek word *sarx*, which is commonly translated as "flesh." In one Scriptural context it means our physical bodies but in another context it means our old selfish, sinful nature. To the extent that we live according to the gratification of our physical senses, to that same extent we are sowing to the flesh. Both Jude and James describe as *sensual* those who live according to their unbridled carnal desires (James 3:15, Jude 19).

Paul urged Spirit indwelt believers to put to death that old way of living where our physical senses dictated our behaviours. "If by the Spirit you put to death the deeds of the body, you will live!" In other words, to enjoy our new life of living under the government of the Spirit, we must exercise self control and disengage from being controlled by our carnal or fleshly desires. This means we cannot walk according to our physical senses and their constant cravings for sensual gratification. Reprobate sinners live continuously according to their carnal desires as they relentlessly feed the lusts of the flesh. But God's holy people are to train themselves to live above the demands of the physical senses for endless gratification. This means abstaining "from fleshly lusts which war against the soul" (1 Peter 2:11) and abstaining "from sexual immorality" (1 Thessalonians 4:3).

To live according to the Spirit, we must break the unholy nexus between body and soul, otherwise our bodies will continually set the agenda. It is widely believed that "the eyes are the window of the soul." But the same could be said for our other physical senses. The sense of touch craves sexual arousal; the sense of taste and smell arouses our physical appetite for food and drink. Many people have been destroyed through their idolatry of food and intoxicants. Paul spoke of those "whose god is their belly" (Philippians 3:19).

Beyond our weakness to continually live to gratify our craving for food, the eyes are the greatest on-ramp for sensual gratification. The eye-gate is the entry point for endless sexual arousal and all kinds of visual media and worldly entertainment. Paul warned explicitly against the idolatry and worship of the human form (Romans 1:25). John warned believers to beware of "the lust of the eyes" (1 John 2:16).

Visual imagery continually bombards our senses, seducing and enticing us to desire all that we see with our eyes. Our thoughts and emotions are so easily swayed by what we see, leading us to make spontaneous choices that we later regret. Pornography addicts feast their eyes continually on imagery that feeds data straight into the mind and the emotions, inevitably creating a psychological and physical dependency on sexual stimulation. But in the same way, a covetous person who craves every material thing that he or she sees with their eyes, can become powerfully addicted to material gratification through the never ending acquisition of material things. Jesus said, "A man's life does not consist in the abundance of his possessions" (Luke 12:15 NIV). Those who mindlessly submit themselves to media advertising live in a continuous state of materialistic arousal, not unlike the porn addict. Covetousness is a form of idolatry and it centres upon the lust of the eyes.

Materialism and sexual seduction continually place a demand upon our souls, arousing desire which evolves into lust. Peter urged believers "to abstain from sinful desires, which war against your soul" (1 Peter 2:11NIV). James outlined the process of the descent from desire to sin: "Each one is tempted when he is drawn away by his own desires and enticed. Then, when desire has conceived, it gives birth to sin" (James 1:14-15). James was vitally concerned with the focus of our desires. He warned against "your desires for pleasure that war in your members"(James 4:1). Carnal desires arise primarily from the things we see. Even Jesus was tempted by the devil through the things that He could see. "The devil took Him to a very high mountain *and showed Him* all the kingdoms of the world and their splendour" (Matthew 4:8 NIV).

Activating Our Spiritual Senses

Spirit empowered self-control switches our focus away from end-less visual stimulation (the things that are seen) to the things that are not seen. Paul said, "For we walk by faith, not by sight" (2 Corinthians 5:7). The new birth gives us the ability to behold invisible things. Jesus said, "I tell you the truth, no one can see the kingdom of God unless he is born again" (John 3:3 NIV). Paul said, "We do not look at the things which are seen, but at the things which are not seen. For the things which are seen are temporary, but the things which are not seen are eternal" (2 Corinthians 4:18). Jesus imparts the gift of spiritual sight so that we are supernaturally empowered to fix our eyes on Him.

But how do we look at the things that are not seen? Paul's answer to this question lies in his revelation of the "eyes of the heart," which are capable of focusing upon those things that are invisible to our natural eyes. "I pray also that the eyes of your heart may be enlight-ened" (Ephesians 1:18 NIV). Ever since Christ made His home in our hearts, the Spirit has been at work to shift our focus away from the lust of our natural eyes in order to train us to fix our eyes on the glory of Jesus. As new creations in Christ, the veil has been removed and we are equipped to behold the glory of the Lord. "But we all, with unveiled face, beholding as in a mirror the glory of the Lord..." (2 Corinthians 3:18).

If we submit to the lust of the eyes, we will be subjected to endless temptation and the possibility that we will fall again and again into the temptations of the world. But if we learn how to use the eyes of our heart to re-focus on the glory of the Lord, we will be transformed! Where is our attention as Christians? There is a world of explosive spiritual activity inside our human spirit now that it has been joined to the Spirit of Christ. Paul said that this new reality is "according to the power [*dunamis*] that works in us" (Ephesians 3:30). This *dunamis* power (from which we derive the word dynamite) is like a supernova that radiates divine energy at the white hot core of our being. David likened the Lord to the sun that shines with radiant splendour: "For the Lord God is a sun and shield" (Psalm 84:11).

Our spirits are now gloriously brimming with the resurrection life of God, and they are fully revived and pulsating with the activity of His "life-giving Spirit" (1 Corinthians 15:45). Paul gloried in the revelation of all "His energy, which so powerfully works in me" (Colossians 1:29 NIV). God is continuously at work energizing our human spirit with His powerful Spirit that raised Christ from the dead. He now wants our souls to be awakened to the reality that there is a Holy Spirit "party" going on inside our spirit. "It is God **who works in you** to will and to act according to His good purpose" (Philippians 2:13 NIV). All His works are marked by a "joy inexpressible and full of glory" (1 Peter 1:8).

God is seeking to flood our spiritual senses with His glory, His love, His peace, and His joy. The soul was never intended to be dominated by the sensory overload that comes through feasting upon the spirit of the world. Rather, our souls were intended to be continuously under the influence and control of the Spirit of God. This is how Jesus lived on earth. His soul was continuously stimulated and energized by the Spirit of God. The interior life of Jesus was continuously flooded with love, peace, and joy. He was infinitely more conscious of the presence of the glory of the Father abiding in His own heart than the seduction and temptations of the world that sought an entry point into His soul. Jesus lived under the relentless sway of a "big tent revival" that never stopped!

The sensory dimension of Jesus' soul was attuned to the glory of God rather than to the world with all its temptations that place a relentless demand upon the human senses. Whilst Jesus was continually conscious of the seduction and temptation of the world He walked in a higher dimension of sensory awareness, because He was attuned to heaven. His heart was permanently awakened to the music of heaven and to the voice of His Father who continuously spoke the word "Beloved" over His heart. The floodgates of His soul were wide open to the overtures of heaven! Jesus modelled the ultimate expression of human life to all who observed the way He lived on earth. His soul was infinitely more attuned to the indwelling Spirit and His power than He was to the world around Him. And this is how we should live our lives!

Supernatural self-control is the key to living in such a way that we are more attuned to the life of Christ within us than the pull of the world upon our outer senses. The great mystics practiced what they called "centering prayer." They turned their focus within: to the indwelling fire of God's presence that burned at the centre of their being. They intentionally pursued a greater unveiling of the beatific vision of the glory of the Lord with the new eyes of the heart. Therefore, a world of divine glory and ecstasy was opened up to their hearts through the fiery activity of the Spirit within. They learned how to open their eyes to heavenly realities in such a way that their souls were flooded by the sensory overload of divine glory. Their thought life was overtaken by the mind of Christ and their emotions were overwhelmed by divine passion and love.

The interior windows of the soul that are focused inwardly upon the indwelling Christ are shaped like a cross. As we say yes to the cross, these inward facing windows of the soul are opened to the light of the glory of God, which floods our senses and elevates our souls in such a way that we are transported into the Spirit. God has always intended that our soul would be continually controlled by our spirit in mystical union with His Spirit so that we learn how to host the very mind, will, and emotions of Jesus through the faculties of our own soul.

John proclaimed that "The One who is in you is greater than the one who is in the world" (1 John 4:4). Another translation says, "The Spirit who lives in you is greater than the spirit who lives in the world" (NLT.) Christ in us is infinitely stronger than the spirit of the world surrounding us. If our mindset is that of a besieged city, relentlessly fending off the marauding army of demonic temptations, we will lose sight of the superiority of the power of the indwelling Spirit of God. One of the greatest keys to the overcoming life comes through nurturing the vision of the supremacy and greatness of God who has taken up permanent residence in the heart of every born again believer. Self-control is a fruit of the indwelling Spirit, but we will only have this fruit if we focus on "Who" is now living inside of us. We are to apply that powerful revelation in a way that brings our interior lives into divine order, establishing the internal government of the Spirit. The challenge for every believer who seeks to live and walk continually in the Spirit is to bring every aspect of our soul into perfect alignment and subjection to our renewed spirit that is comprehensively immersed in the Spirit of the Lord.

Chapter Fifteen

I Will Pour Out My Spirit

The goal of Christian discipleship is the development of Christlikeness in every single area of our lives. Jesus said that the essence of being a disciple is in becoming just like our Master (Matthew 10:25). When we reflect on the life of Jesus, there is one word that encapsulates everything that Jesus was about: love. John tells us that God is love. And Jesus was God manifest in the flesh. He was love incarnate. Every aspect of Jesus expressed the Father's love – every word that proceeded from His lips and every action that He performed, right down to every nuance of His facial expression. Everything about Jesus revealed the supernatural love of God. And then Jesus tells us that love must be the defining attribute of His true disciples (John 13:35). Jesus' disciples must also become an expression of the Father's love.

The supernatural love that flows out of the heart of God is described by a unique Greek word: *agape*. The distinguishing quality of this agape love of God is the way it is poured out upon others. Love has to look like something. Genuine, unfeigned love is tangibly felt. It is demonstrated in a tangible way. The nature of agape love is a self-sacrificial love that elevates others and pours itself out in a way that those who are the recipients of this love actually feel loved and cared for. Divine love pursues others. It is not passive but radically proactive. Love pursues, and love gives relentlessly. It flows like a river out of God's heart. It never runs dry and it never fails. It just keeps on pouring out. In the book of Joel, God made a prophetic promise that became one of the better known verses of the Old Testament because it defined the advent of the New Covenant. God said, "It shall come to pass afterward that I will pour out My Spirit on all flesh; your sons and your daughters shall prophesy, your old men shall dream dreams, your young men shall see visions. And also on My menservants and on My maidservants I will pour out My Spirit in those days" (Joel 2:28-29).

This prophetic promise of the outpouring of the Holy Spirit was gloriously fulfilled on the Day of Pentecost. Peter quoted this Scripture from Joel to explain to the crowd what was happening. We are all extremely familiar with the phrase, "I will pour out my Spirit." But in this chapter I want you to see it from a different perspective. This was God pouring out "His *Spirit*" upon His people. Jesus said, "God is spirit, and those who worship Him must worship in spirit and truth" (John 4:24 NIV). God is a spirit being! When God pours out His spirit, He is pouring His very Self out. He is not pouring out a commodity or a product, He is pouring Himself out upon whoever is rightly positioned to receive Him. The right position is an open, hungry heart that is waiting on the Lord to receive the fullness of everything He wants to pour out upon us.

The point that I want to make is that God pours Himself out on us because God is love. Love pours out! That is the very nature of love: to pours itself out on another. God is love! That is why He created our hearts: to have sons and daughters that He could pour out His love upon. It is the very nature of God to look for hearts that are hungry to receive from Him. He cannot stay away when He finds wholehearted people who have a genuine heart for God. He relentlessly pours everything out upon the receptive, hungry heart. "Now hope does not disappoint, because the love of God has been poured out in our hearts by the Holy Spirit who was given to us" (Romans 5:5).

By now you may have guessed where this is going. We have spent much of this book focusing upon the human spirit, which is a finite replication of the spirit of God. God is a spirit. He has a soul (mind, will, and emotions) but in His essential being, Jesus revealed that God is a spirit. We are comprehensively made in the image and likeness of God. Jesus even went as far as saying we are gods. He said, "Is it not written in your law, 'I said, "You are gods?"'" (John 10:34). This is undoubtedly one of the hardest verses in the whole Bible.

New-agers grab a hold of these words of Jesus, wrench them out of their biblical context, tread beneath their feet the biblical world-view and seek to assert that the whole of humanity is divine. They say that if there is a God, then human beings are God. The presence of New Age deception makes Christians extremely uncomfortable about this verse, so we try to argue that Jesus wasn't really saying what it sounds like He was saying. But Jesus was quoting a Psalm where the Lord Himself said, "You are gods and all of you are children of the Most High" (Psalm 82:6). The Hebrew word for "gods" is *elohim,* which means either "God" (singular) or "gods" (plural).

When God said, "You shall have no other gods before Me," the Hebrew word for "gods" was also *elohim* (Exodus 20:3). We see the word being used in a singular sense in relation to the Most High God, but also in a plural sense where it always refers to created be-ings, whether they were demonic beings or human beings created in the image of God. The Lord revealed that the "gods" that the heathen worshipped were actually demons. "They sacrificed to demons, which are not God – gods [*elohim*] they had not known, gods that recently appeared, gods your fathers did not fear" (Deuteronomy 32:17 NIV). When Jesus audaciously told the Pharisees "you are gods," He was telling them that they were intrinsically godlike, yet without being the one true God. Of course Jesus was not telling these people that they were God! That would contradict the entire biblical worldview. Rather, Jesus was highlighting the extraordinary nature of human beings: finite beings yet made in the exact similitude of the infinite God who is also a spirit.

There is a unique godlike quality to human beings. God is a spirit and we are also spirit beings, albeit clothed in flesh and blood. Nevertheless, we are spirit beings. Your human spirit was made to glow. It was never made to be a black hole that was fundamentally selfish, self-focused, and narcissistic in character. That is a hideous distortion of everything that human beings were made by God to be. Our spirit has been created to never die. It was made to shine like a bright star, joined to the Spirit of God Himself, radiating the glory of God. But the fall of man caused us to fall a million miles short of the glory of God.

When Adam and Eve sinned their human spirit passed from life to death; they fell from being bright and glorious stars to being vacuous black holes. Our polarity was fully reversed and we became narcissistic beings, focused only on ourselves and descending into the abyss of self worship and utter selfishness. This selfish orientation is the very essence of sin and death. A sinful person is a self-centred person, whereas a righteous person is a Christ-centred person.

The miracle of the new creation is that our spirit is now gloriously and comprehensively renewed, fully immersed in, and joined to the Spirit of Christ. The moment God made your spirit new by raising it from the dead you were no longer a black hole; you were restored to that pristine condition that existed before the fall where humans once shone like stars in the universe (Philippians 2:15 NIV). Now that our spirit is in His Spirit, we have been plunged into the heavenly culture of love. God has made a way for you and me to pour out our spirit just as God pours out His spirit. Inside of you is an unlimited reservoir of supernatural agape love. Your spirit is no longer selfish and trapped in the gravitational pull of darkness and blackness. It is now full of light and capable of shining.

God is seeking to train us in the new lifestyle of agape love. Graham Cooke, in his excellent book, *Manifesting Your Spirit*, writes:

> Manifesting your spirit is a spiritual discipline. The Holy Spirit is constantly seeking to cause our inner man of the spirit to rise up and manifest itself in the course of everyday life.[22]

The first step in manifesting your spirit is to allow the Spirit of revelation to unveil your new nature and to fully convince you that you are a new creation in Christ. But there are issues that we need to deal with inside our heart that can block the flow of this explosive love. Bitterness, unforgiveness, anger, malice, and judgmentalism – all of these fruits of the old carnal nature have a way of dominating the landscape of our heart and eclipsing the radiant love of God that has been restored to our spirit. Watchman Nee, in his famous book, *Release of the Spirit*, explores the power of the cross to put to death everything in our heart that would prevent the light and love of Christ from radiating out of our innermost being.

There is an art to pouring out your spirit, and God, who relentlessly pours out His spirit, wants to train you in the lost art of releasing, manifesting, or pouring out your human spirit. Jesus promised that living waters will flow out of your innermost being (John 7:38). It is your destiny to shine like the sun. To live consistently with the reality of who we are as new creations we must press in to that place where we learn how to shine. There is a combinational effect of biblical revelation, which continually unveils the new creation miracle in order to awaken the reality of who we are, and the power of alignment with the cross as we bring everything inside our heart under the resurrection power of the crucified life. When these two realities are combined through faith, it releases an explosion of divine life within us, which unlocks the flow of God's amazing love. This is what it means to walk in love: to release what is inside of us so that it powerfully flows through a crucified life.

Paul said, "Live a life of love, just as Christ loved us and gave Himself up for us as a fragrant offering and sacrifice to God" (Ephesians 5:2 NIV). Love leads us to give our life up and to lay our life down. "By this we know love, because He laid down His life for us. And we also ought to lay down our lives for the brethren" (1 John 3:16). There is an intentionality embedded in the very nature of agape love. This is no ordinary kind of earthly love; this is divine love that compels us to pursue other human beings and to pour ourselves into others. "For the love of Christ compels us" (2 Corinthians 5:14). It begins by making a decree over our own life. God wants to train us to wholeheartedly say, "I will pour out my spirit!" I was made for love and I was made to find my ultimate identity in the deepest expression of conformity to the heart of Christ who laid His life down for us.

Love leads us to the cross. The cross is the ultimate expression of love in the universe. There is no greater love than to lay our life down for others. God wants to establish the cross in our heart just as the cross has always been established in the heart of God. To live for love means we must be dead to everything that exalts itself as the enemy of love. The cross is infinitely deeper than a singular historical event two thousand years ago when Christ was suspended between heaven and earth. The cross is an existential reality that has always existed in the heart of God. It was played out for all the world to see as God commended His love toward us in the cross. If we say yes to love, we must also say yes to the cross. It is through the miracle of the cross that we can now say, "I will pour out my spirit just as the God of love relentlessly pours out His spirit!"

God cannot do this for you. I'm sure He wishes He could, but He knows there is only one person who can put the key in the lock and open the door. He gives us everything we need in terms of resources, strength, strong revelation, and relentless encouragement, but at the end of the day, He cannot do *for you* what He has purposed that He will only do *through you* and in complete cooperation with you. He continually *works in* us to impart to us the willingness and the power to be transformed but we must *work out* our own salvation in humility before Him. Paul put it so beautifully and poetically when he said, "Therefore, my beloved, as you have always obeyed ... *work out* your own salvation with fear and trembling; for it is God who *works in* you both to will and to do for His good pleasure" (Philippians 2:12-13).

God invites us into the mystery of the cosmic dance between divine love and the power of the cross. These two ultimate realities are utterly inseparable in the heart of God. God wants to re-connect these two powerful realities in the human heart in order to transition us from the depths of our brokenness back to a place of authentic wholeness and healthy integration in our hearts. All this is all done at the meeting place of love and the cross as our hearts are conformed to the likeness of His beautiful heart.

Chapter Sixteen

The Warfare Surrounding the New Creation

Infinitely greater progress would be made in the journey of heart transformation were it not for the reality of the powers of darkness and their relentless spiritual warfare against the saints. The revelation of the spiritual battle that rages around the soul of every born again believer is a reality check for each of us in our quest to be transformed from glory to glory. It goes without saying that the devil and his army of billions of demons are profoundly threatened by the saints of God taking a hold of their new identity in Christ and rising up into a stature of greatness in the earth. Every believer in Christ has the potential to release the glory of Christ to the same extent as did Smith Wigglesworth, Amy Semple McPherson, or someone even greater. Therefore, the combined powers of darkness have launched an all-out offensive against believers in order to hinder their spiritual growth and to take them out of the race.

The presence of the powers of darkness on the earth exercise a tempering influence upon our personal spiritual transformation, because the enemy of our souls has a number of tactical advantages over new believers. Not least of these advantages is his depth of experience that he has acquired over the past twenty centuries in his relentless war upon New Testament saints. He is a seasoned campaigner and a brilliant strategist who scans the life and scrutinises the soul of every new follower of Christ in order to develop a customised strategy to bring about our downfall and to promote our demise. Whenever the devil identifies a point of weakness, he unleashes all the hosts of hell against it. The devil seeks to bring about the utter destruction of believers with infinite spiritual potential. Paul warned every Christian of the ever-present danger that "Satan should take advantage of us" (2 Corinthians 2:11). Paul's remedy was to argue that we, as a community of faith, "are not ignorant of his devices" (2 Corinthians 2:11).

The problem is that every new babe in Christ is often ignorant of the devil's schemes and devices. It is deeply unfortunate, but true, that many new believers are not saved into a spiritual environment where they are equipped in spiritual warfare and made aware of the devil's subtle strategies and schemes. If the devil can discourage and disorient a new believer in the early months or years of his or her new relationship with Christ, there is significant potential to completely eliminate yet one more person who has the propensity to become a mighty warrior in the kingdom of God.

Peter warned believers, "Be sober, be vigilant; because your adversary the devil walks about like a roaring lion, seeking whom he may devour. Resist him, steadfast in the faith, knowing that the same sufferings are experienced by your brotherhood in the world" (1 Peter 5:8-9). Every brother and sister in Christ is subjected to this relentless assault from the kingdom of darkness. Even if we are not persecuted by people, we are nevertheless continually persecuted by the devil and his demons. Without a good foundation, weak believers are extremely vulnerable to the persecution of the world of dark spirits. Jesus warned, "When trouble or persecution comes because of the word, he quickly falls away" (Matthew 13:21 NIV).

This may sound rather gloomy, but it is sad but true that there are many "stillborn" believers who come to Christ with a shaky foundation and quickly become discouraged and disappointed when the

Christian life doesn't seem to immediately deliver on its promise of unlimited peace, love, and joy. One remedy to this high rate of attrition is to train new believers from day one in the art of defensive spiritual warfare.

New Christians need to be told straight up that turning to Christ may result in hostile opposition from family and friends. But even if someone's choice to follow Christ is met with great celebration by friends and family, there is still hostile opposition from the enemy of our souls. Every new Christian desperately needs to be equipped for the avalanche of persecution that will inevitably come upon them from the invisible realm of principalities and powers.

The warfare that surrounds the life of every believer is waged exclusively in the arena of the soul. The spirit of the believer is a sanctuary of peace and rest from the turmoil of battle. Jesus told us to "go into your room, and when you have shut the door, pray to your Father who is in the secret place; and your Father who sees in secret will reward you openly" (Matthew 6:6). The secret place of the Most High God is now inside every believer. It is called the "secret place" because the enemy doesn't know where it is! God has made provision for us to hide in the secret place, away from the intensity of the storm that rages around us. Outside of our inner sanctuary the battle rages and the devil uses every possible strategy to persuade us to give up on Jesus. He scans us to gauge our greatest weakness and then he assigns as many demons as necessary to wear us out so we give into temptation. When he scans a believer, he scrutinises their soul to find a point of entry. He examines our relationships, our thought life, our words, our choices, our actions, and our feelings to look for the specific area to target in his evil plan to rob, kill, and destroy.

The theatre of battle is the mind, the will, the emotions, and the physical body. All of us who have followed Christ for any length of time would realise the intensity of the battle that rages in and around our thought life. The mind is a major battlefield, especially as the human mind, left totally to its own devices in the world, quickly descends into entrenched patterns of negativity. There is so much for the devil to feed upon in a new believer whose mind has been completely unguarded for however many years they have previously been living in the darkness. The "carnal mind," as Paul called it, is riddled with negativity and negative self talk. When we first come to Christ, our minds are filled with fears, doubts, lies, perverse thoughts, worry, confusion, depression, and judgments toward others.

Satan knows how to infiltrate a person's mind and ride on the back of all of the negativity and darkness of the mind. He will seek to capitalise upon our pessimistic and bleak thoughts for all they are worth! Similarly, the battle also rages in the arena of the emotions. Satan loves to ride on the back of anger, resentment, bitterness, unforgiveness, lust, judgmentalism, fear, shame, guilt, and depression – the list goes on and on. All of our dark and destructive emotions are fair game for our merciless adversary who seeks to gain maximum leverage from feelings that have not yet seen the light of day.

Oftentimes, we are not even aware of the full extent of our broken emotions that lurk beneath the surface. Our denial, our emotional detachment, and in the worse case, our total dissociation can make us extremely vulnerable as inexperienced believers to comprehend what the devil is doing as he plays with our negative feelings toward ourselves and others, just like a cat plays with a mouse.

Our choices are another major arena of spiritual warfare. God has blessed us with the power of choice but this power to choose has been massively compromised through humanity's fall into sin. We can't just "choose" not to sin, otherwise the world would be a much better place, even apart from the grace of God. The truth is that people become locked into sinful habits and patterns of sinful choices because the more they yield to the power of sin the more they become enslaved to sin. The addict may desire to be free from addictive behaviours, but without the grace of God empowering him or her, the relentless surrender to temptation seems like a tragic merry-go-round that never stops.

When someone first comes to Christ their will is often comprehensively trashed and there is a significant struggle to learn how to make godly choices. In predictable style, the devil rides upon our decimated capacity to choose righteousness. He constantly seeks to hold us in captivity to sin by exploiting our fallen will to maximum effect. It is only through a raw act of grace-empowered repentance that "they may come to their senses and escape the snare of the devil, having been taken captive by him to do his will" (2 Timothy 2:26).

The same is true for our physical body. Ask any addict who turns to Christ how strong the physical cravings are for another hit of heroin, another cigarette, another drink, or another one-night-stand with a fellow sex addict. Those who have relentlessly yielded their bodies to sin and unrighteousness for decades find themselves in a major battle to break patterns of addictive behaviours. Paul gives a lengthy exhortation to believers to train themselves to yield their bodies to righteousness, instead of unrighteousness, so that the devil cannot control their bodies any longer.

> Do not let sin control the way you live; do not give in to its lustful desires. Do not let any part of your body become a tool of wickedness, to be used for sinning. Instead, give yourselves completely to God since you have been given new life. And use your whole body as a tool to do what is right for the glory of God. Sin is no longer your master, for you are no longer subject to the law, which enslaves you to sin. Instead, you are free by God's grace. So since God's grace has set us free from the law, does this mean we can go on sinning? Of course not! Don't you realize that whatever you choose to obey becomes your master? You can choose sin, which leads to death, or you can choose to obey God and receive his approval. Thank God! Once you were slaves of

sin, but now you have obeyed with all your heart the new teaching God has given you. Now you are free from sin, your old master, and you have become slaves to your new master, righteousness. I speak this way, using the illustration of slaves and masters, because it is easy to understand. Before, you let yourselves be slaves of impurity and lawlessness. Now you must choose to be slaves of righteousness so that you will become holy. In those days, when you were slaves of sin, you weren't concerned with doing what was right. And what was the result? It was not good, since now you are ashamed of the things you used to do, things that end in eternal doom. But now you are free from the power of sin and have become slaves of God. Now you do those things that lead to holiness and result in eternal life. For the wages of sin is death, but the free gift of God is eternal life through Christ Jesus our Lord. (Romans 6:12 -23 NLT)

The New King James Version uses a more archaic turn of phrase, drawing the distinction between yielding our bodies to either righteousness or unrighteousness: "Therefore do not let sin reign in your mortal body, that you should obey it in its lusts. And do not present your members as instruments of unrighteousness to sin, but present yourselves to God as being alive from the dead, and your members as instruments of righteousness to God" (Romans 6:12-13). Satan deliberately seeks to gain control over our physical bodies. To this end he relentlessly barrages believers with temptation in the hope that they will surrender to the pressure and stay in patterns of habitual bondage to sin. He takes advantage of a strong physical desire for gratification and capitalises upon the physical cravings of weak believers.

Of course, none of this is particularly good news. It is a stark reality check right on the heels of the good news that Christ has done such a marvellous work in miraculously regenerating our human spirit so that He can take up residence in the heart of His people. The one consolation in this dark narrative of human brokenness is the fact that God's power, His truth, and His love is infinitely stronger than the power of the devil's lies and ability to keep people bound in chains of darkness. Of course, the powers of darkness are no match for the power of Christ. It is inevitable that God will make us more than conquerors if we continue to purpose in our hearts to follow Christ and learn the art of engaging in spiritual warfare. When the Holy Spirit first comes into our hearts, He really goes for it!

He is the Spirit of Truth, and He loves to shatter every lie of the evil one. It really is amazing how much a new believer learns in the first few months of following Jesus. As long as a new believer remains hungry for the truth, this "honeymoon season" can be a season of extraordinary spiritual growth and breakthrough.

Demonisation and the Christian

The other major arena of warfare for the new believer is the reality that the devil has the capability to extend considerable demonic influence over the strongholds of the mind, will, emotions, and the physical body. There has been a vigorous debate in Christian circles about the devil's ability to "possess" Christians. Most Christians recoil at the notion of the demonic possession of the believer. We are God's "purchased possession" (Ephesians 1:14), so how can we simultaneously be the possession of a demon. But for all the references in the New Testament to "demon possession" it often comes as a surprise to Christians that the term is a misnomer. The Greek word is *daimonizomai* and an infinitely better way of translating this word is to use the English transliteration: demonized. Demonization shifts the concept out of the arena of "possession" and into the arena of degrees of influence. Now, if we ask the question: can a Christian come under a measure of demonic influence, the answer would universally be a resounding "Yes!"

If a Christian has significant strongholds in their life that they are still under, they make themselves vulnerable to an ongoing degree of demonic influence in the arena of the soul. Demons cannot touch the spirit of a born again believer but they can legally touch any area of the soul that is still actively under the influence of sin and spiritual darkness. To the extent that a Christian traffics in spiritual darkness, to that same extent they are vulnerable to demonization. If they have given themselves over to any area of sin or emotional brokenness, either before their conversion to Christ, or subsequent to their conversion, these are areas where the devil has a legal loophole to violate and influence the Christian. Sin, rebellion, and disobedience are all part of the dominion of darkness. The key New Testament passage that indicates this degree of demonic influence in the lives of disobedient Christians is found in Ephesians 2.

> And you He made alive, who were dead in trespasses and sins, in which you once walked according to the course of this world, according to the prince of the power of the air, ***the spirit who now works in the sons of disobedience,*** among whom also we all once conducted ourselves in the lusts of our flesh, fulfilling the desires of the flesh and of the mind, and were by nature children of wrath, just as the others. (Ephesians 2:1-3)

I have deliberately highlighted a key phrase in this text. Satan is revealed as "the spirit that currently works [*energeo*] in the sons of disobedience." The "sons of disobedience" is a designation for unbelievers, not Christians. The important thing to note is that the devil, and by implication the entire demonic realm, have the capacity to "energise" those who engage in any kind of disobedience to God. So, for example, if a Christian has an ongoing problem with pornography and they have not been able to break the addiction even though they have been following Jesus for years, their ongoing disobedience leaves them wide open to a level of demonic influence (demonization).

Similarly, in the arena of the emotions, if a Christian who has been abused by their non-Christian spouse allows a stronghold of resentment or bitterness to enter their soul they are equally vulnerable to demons energising them in their bitterness. What does a demonically energised believer look like? On the surface they may look like a regular church-going believer, but if they were to pursue ministry for their problem with a Christian counsellor or pastor with an anointing for deliverance there may be some interesting fireworks especially when the glory of the Lord shows up in the ministry time!

My wife and I have been in pastoral ministry for decades and we have an active deliverance ministry with Christians who, for various-reasons, have not been able to break through their personal problems. We have cast out hundreds of demons over the past fifteen years since the Lord led us into deliverance ministry. All of this ministry has been with committed Christians who have had ongoing struggles with various expressions of disobedience, either unforgiveness in the emotional arena or some degree of rebellion in the volitional arena.

We have been astonished to see many Christians who have breakthrough in some areas of their life begin to manifest real demons as we have laid hands upon them and have soaked them in the presence of the Lord. We have engaged in some high level deliverance with people we know personally who are very committed to following Jesus!

This has been a startling revelation of the ability of the powers of darkness to occupy areas of the body and the soul of Christians who have not fully appreciated the reality that they have been playing with fire by entertaining sin or by allowing emotional issues to continue to dominate their personal lives. Satan is a legalist who looks for legal loopholes to harass and torment genuine believers who foolishly traffic in spiritual darkness. He really does go around like a roaring lion seeking whom he may devour. The regeneration of the believer is nothing short of a glorious miracle. But we need to be aware that there are a whole set of factors that mitigate against Christians breaking through into a place of victory and strength.

These factors temper our expectations, thereby allowing us to minister grace to weak believers. There is nothing more difficult to bear than uncompassionate brothers and sisters in Christ who place expectations and demands upon their brethren to be in a place of victory when they themselves haven't done the hard work of learning the principles of being an overcomer. If Christians are still overwhelmed by certain strongholds, they need loving brothers and sisters to come alongside them who can encourage them and show them how to overcome.

Jesus is compassionate and understanding, and He knows each of us inside out. He has a comprehensive knowledge of our personal journey and the complexities of our own hearts. While He doesn't tolerate sin, He appreciates that our entanglement in sin, darkness, demonic influence, and deep-level emotional brokenness are mitigating factors that often continue to hold us in bondage. Rather than condemning the struggling brother or sister, Jesus comes alongside us as an Advocate, continually calling us out of sin and brokenness. As much as we want to see a victorious church filled with gloriously victorious Christians, the reality is that for many Christians the journey back to holiness and wholeness is a long, hard road.

Paul gives some good advice to Christians who have a propensity to judge their brothers and sisters because of their personal struggles: "You, then, why do you judge your brother? Or why do you look down on your brother? We who are strong ought to bear with the failings of the weak" (Romans 14:10; 15:1 NIV). True spirituality shows compassion and gentleness toward those who are struggling. "Brothers, if someone is caught in a sin, you who are spiritual should restore him gently. But watch yourself, or you also may be tempted" (Galatians 6:1 NIV).

As a pastor, I work a lot with genuine strugglers. Our church has a street ministry to people with major addiction problems. While we want to see people experience breakthrough, we have also had to learn how to be gracious and patient, because God has been extremely gracious and patient with us. God just keeps on calling out the treasure and relentlessly encouraging us to overcome.

He points us to the revelation of His power to overcome and He calls out the reality that we are new creations. He loves us into a place of wholeness and holiness by continually overwhelming us with the revelation of His kindness. And we are learning to do the same by revealing how great, loving, and kind God is.

Endnotes

1. John W. Peterson, *Heaven Came Down,* © 1961

2. U2, "Magnificent", © Polygram International Music Publications 2009

3. See Phil Mason, *Quantum Glory: The Science of Heaven Invading Earth*, (XP Media Phoenix, Arizona USA 2012)

4. *Hebrews: IVP New Testament Commentary*, Ray C. Stedman (IVP 1992)

5. Ibid p.97

6. Ibid p.98

7. Graham Cooke, *Towards a Powerful Inner Life*. pp. 20-21(Sovereign World 2003)

8. Ray C. Stedman, *How To Live What You Believe: A Life Related Study in Hebrews*, (Regal Books 1997) pp. 53-54

9. Watchman Nee, *The Release of the Spirit*, (Sure Foundation Publishers 2000), pp. 10-11

10. Part of verse 10: "an exceeding great army" is from the NKJV not the NIV.

11. A. W. Tozer, *The Knowledge of the Holy,* (Harper One 1978)

12. Graham Cooke, *The Nature of God* (Sovereign World 2003)

13. Pneumatology is the doctrine of the Holy Spirit. Gordon Fee is the author of *God's Empowering Presence; the Holy Spirit in the Letters of Paul*. The book is a 992 page comprehensive treatment of every verse in the Pauline corpus dealing with the doctrine of the Holy Spirit.

14. Unless we regard Ephesians 4:4-6 as a formulae of Spirit Baptism: "There is one body and one Spirit, just as you were called in one hope of your calling; one Lord, one faith, one baptism; one God and Father of all, who is above all, and through all, and in you all."

15. http://melodygreen.com/Articles/1000008648/Last_Days_Ministries/LDM/Discipleship_Teachings/Who_Will_You.aspx

16. Raniero Cantalamessa, *Sober Intoxication of the Spirit: Filled with the Fullness of God* (Servant Books 2005) pp.2-3

17. ibid

18. ibid

19. ibid pp. 4-5

20. Jerry Bridges, *The Practice of Godliness*, (Nav Press 1996), pp. 148-49

21. Graham Cooke, *Toward a Powerful Inner Life*, (Sovereign World 2003), pp. 20 -21

22. Graham Cooke, *Manifesting Your Spirit*, (Brilliant Book House 2010), pp.5,11

New Earth Tribe

Phil and Maria Mason are the Spiritual Directors of **New Earth Tribe**, a spiritual community that began in 1998 and is located in Byron Bay, Australia. Since 2006, this community has experienced a sustained outpouring of supernatural ministry. Byron Bay is world renowned as a centre of New Age spirituality. As Phil and Maria tell it, "Finding ourselves in the midst of the New Age marketplace, we have developed a passion to penetrate the culture with the supernatural healing power of Christ. As we have pressed into this goal, we have experienced a significant outpouring of healing, which has released an ecstatic atmosphere over our community. The more we live in the atmosphere of the supernatural, the more we are elevated into a state of spiritual ecstasy – and we were made for ecstasy!

Whenever Jesus healed the sick, those who witnessed the miracles were astonished and amazed. Jesus called these miracles signs and wonders. They were tangible signs of the invasion of the kingdom of heaven that induced a sense of astonishment, joy, and wonder. Revival culture is sustained by a continued outpouring of these signs and wonders, much like the community of believers in the book of Acts. The outpouring of the Spirit is always accompanied by an outpouring of authentic joy and ecstasy.

The greatest core values of the Tribe are community and intimacy. We have been on a fourteen-year journey into spiritual community, and we are finding more and more that true fulfilment in God is only enjoyed in the context of committed relationships. Any good fruit that has come out of our community is a result of an unswerving commitment to real, accountable friendships that are both loving and truthful. We truly love the power of community and we wholeheartedly preach it as the foundation for lasting revival.

Our journey has also seen an explosion of wild worship and unique creativity that has accompanied the outpouring of the supernatural. We are committed to the journey of becoming an authentic "Book of Acts" community in the 21st century that turns the world upside down!

To find out more about this community, please visit our website:

www.newearthtribe.com

DEEP END SCHOOL OF THE SUPERNATURAL

Phil and Maria are the directors and founders of the **Deep End School of the Supernatural**. This nine month, part-time school, founded in 2003, trains people of all ages in the Kingdom Ministry of Jesus Christ. One of the unique features of this ministry is the importance placed upon contextualisation. Students are trained to understand New Age and Post-modern culture and to develop an intelligent response to the explosion of this culture. Students develop a model of ministry that takes into account the unique challenges created by the emergence of radical postmodernism with its categorical rejection of absolute truth. Oftentimes Christian ministry in the twenty-first century lacks this contextualisation of the gospel.

The Deep End School is empowered by a specific ministry philosophy. The shift from the modernist era to the post-modernist era represents a transition away from words that describe reality to the subjective experience of reality. We are now living in a "show me" generation, rather than a "tell me" generation. As a result, people are fatigued by a "word only" approach to marketing spirituality. They want to see tangible demonstrations of the world we are attempting to describe.

We have found that the kingdom ministry of Christ is the key to penetrating the hearts of post-modern seekers. Post-modernists have been awakened to the reality of supernatural power and spiritual experience. Subsequently, the Deep End School trains students to heal the sick, break demonic bondages, heal broken hearts, and flow in the prophetic. As an extension of this approach to ministry, the school trains its students to release the glory realm of heaven through true, supernatural encounters with God that usher people into the ecstasy realm.

Post-modern seekers are hungry for authentic spiritual encounters that open up the realm of ecstasy and bliss. That is why they are flocking to New Age practitioners who offer their adherents an experience of supernatural power. New Age and post-modern seekers intentionally bypass expressions of spirituality that cannot deliver an encounter. It is time to give this generation an encounter with the living God. He will rise up a generation of ecstatic lovers of Christ.

To find out more about this nine month school, please visit our website:

www.deependschool.com

Other Books by Phil Mason

Quantum Glory: The Science of Heaven Invading Earth

Quantum Glory explores the intriguing intersection between the two realities of quantum mechanics and the glory of God. Part one of the book explores how the sub-atomic world is a revelation of exceptionally intricate divine design that unveils the mind of our Creator. In part two, the author explains exactly how the glory of God invades our physical universe to affect miracles of divine healing. This book is packed with revelation that is guaranteed to blow your mind. But more than that, it is designed to equip you in supernatural ministry so that you can also release the glory of God on earth as it is in heaven!

The real glory of this book is that it gives understanding of this wonderful world around us in a way that creates awe for what God has done. It also ignites praise in our hearts to the Creator of all, while at the same time giving us understanding of how things work. God left His message everywhere for anyone interested in truth. His fingerprints are everywhere: from the largest galaxies in existence, to the smallest thing known to man. I appreciate Phil's amazing insights and deep understanding of very difficult subjects addressed in **Quantum Glory**. I am especially thankful for his gift of taking big thoughts and breaking them down so that all of us can understand them. But I am also glad for how He values mystery. Anything that creates awe and wonder, all the while pointing to Jesus, to me is priceless. With that note, I highly recommend **Quantum Glory**. Enjoy. Be awed. Give God praise over and over again.

Bill Johnson
Senior Pastor, Bethel Church, Redding, California USA

God is still creating ways for His people to respond to His overtures. All creation speaks of Him and the language and principles of quantum physics are a vital part of His heavenly discourse with humanity. From quantum non-locality through sound waves, string theory, the mathematical order of nature, quantum geometry and the golden ratio, to the alignment between quantum physics and the supernatural, the glory of God and the key to miracles; you will understand more about the radiant nature of God in this book than in any other tome that is specifically non-specific. I heartily recommend Phil Mason to you as a leader in the field of modern day spirituality, the new sciences and the supernatural gospel of the Lord Jesus Christ.

Graham Cooke,
Author, Prophetic Speaker and Owner of Brilliant Book House.com

We are in the midst of a worldwide move of God with signs and wonders breaking out all over the world. In **Quantum Glory,** Phil Mason combines his passion for the science of quantum physics with his personal wealth of experience in supernatural ministry and sound Biblical theology. The result is an explosive mix of revelation that has the potential to powerfully envision and activate you to alter the very fabric of the physical world around you through the healing ministry of Christ. This book fills a vital gap in the literature that is emerging in this present wave of revival.

Dr. Che Ahn
President, Harvest International Ministry
International Chancellor, Wagner Leadership Institute

The Supernatural Transformation Series

If you have enjoyed reading this book, Phil Mason has also written three additional volumes on the theme of the Supernatural Transformation of the Heart. This series outlines a supernatural Kingdom Ministry based model of personal transformation. God seeks to transform our hearts from the inside out as we embrace the call to a deep heart journey of intimacy with God and one another in spiritual community.

This profound theology of the heart puts in place all the conceptual building blocks for deep, personal transformation. It begins with the miracle of the new creation and it unfolds the process of transformation from one degree of glory to another as we allow God to demolish every stronghold of the mind, will, and emotions so that we can be gloriously transformed into the very image of Christ. The context of this transformation is spiritual community that values genuine supernatural encounter with Christ.

Volume 1: The Knowledge of the Heart

Volume 2: The New Creation Miracle

Volume 3: The Heart Journey

Volume 4: The Glory of God and Supernatural Transformation

CONTACT INFORMATION:

www.philmason.org

Phil's website also contains a large selection of his unique teaching materials with downloadable mp3s, individual CDs, CD sets, and DVDs, which can be ordered through his store. PayPal, Master Card, and Visa Card facilities are available for safe online transactions. We ship worldwide. Additional postage and shipping charges apply.

Australia and New Zealand: Please order books through this website. To obtain bulk quantities for bookstores, please contact Phil Mason by writing to: Phil Mason, PO Box 1627, Byron Bay, New South Wales, Australia, 2481 or contact the author by email at: sales@philmason.org

ORDERING INFORMATION

Additional copies of this book and other resources
by Phil Mason as well as other XP Publishing books,
are available at the "store" at XPministries.com, Amazon,
and your local Christian store, upon request.

Wholesale prices for stores and ministries

Please contact:
usaresource@xpministries.com.

In Canada, please contact:
resource@xpministries.com.

Australia and New Zealand:
www.philmason.org
(Please see complete information on page 236).

XP Publishing books are also available to
wholesale and retail stores through
anchordistributors.com

www.XPpublishing.com
XP Ministries